TRUTH Etc.

Fred Dewey—editing and design
Denis Mair (China), Anthony Seidman (Mexico)—contributing editors
Pablo Capra—editorial assistant

This book is an edition of *Beyond Baroque Magazine*
and is published by Beyond Baroque Foundation &
Literary / Arts Center, 681 Venice Blvd., Venice, CA 90291.

The excerpt from *Electric Flesh* included with permission of
Soft Skull Press, NY, NY.

This book was published with the support of The Annenberg
Foundation, the City of Los Angeles Dept. of Cultural Affairs,
The Lawrence Lipton Trust, and our members.

ISBN #1-892184-22-2
Printed in Los Angeles by Fine Arts Printing.

Submissions: Send to the address above with an SASE
for reply only. Written works cannot be returned. Turnaround
time varies. Original visual works will be returned if return
postage and proper return package is provided.

Beyond Baroque
Vol. 28, No. 2

TRUTH Etc.

Contents

For Gary Webb, Hunter S. Thompson, and H.R. Shapiro

THE POET AND ARTIST IN A TIME OF LIES

We face a baroque order of perilous dimensions: truths of philosophy, truths of science, truths of religion, and truths of culture have seemingly aligned themselves
against truth itself. Despite evidence to the contrary, organization lies behind this,
churning outward from the yawning heights of society. The dignity and truth-telling
power of the people is thwarted from every direction by a system that has lost all its
bearings. While the political organization of society grows more mad and dictatorial
by the hour, actuality falls further and further behind; proofs generated for the sake
of fiction and unreality gather and spread. We fight, we resist, but our compass and
opposition are missing.

Something must be retrieved, something must be recovered, something must be
sustained if, at the most basic level, truth and fact are to again to find gentle harbor
in our lives. It is in such times, when truth is hunted down and buried in broad daylight, that artists and poets play an especially important role, less to establish truth
than protect our relation to it, to preserve truth as a journey or search never finished
but that, by its continuation, secures what matters and is significant. When truth and
fact have no anchor, processes move forward senselessly and without understanding.
This is why, after decades if not centuries of progress, barbarism outpaces us, placing
the human mind itself at risk. American society seems to have synchronized and
coordinated itself against truth. It has done so not as previous systems and movements did but with its unique, aw-shucks, jus' your pardner or I'll blow you away
mentality. Our society seems to thrive now on the lie and the energy lying throws off;
the people, unaware the problem is structural, are asked to bear the brunt of it. Voices
arise here and there, but truth-tellers are disappeared. Nothing lasts, and it's on to the
next viral cliché, word, image, or object. Such a dictatorship is new, full of pleasing
fictions, generating destruction to every horizon. The incredible tenacity of the lie
seems to have nothing determined enough to answer it.

When the political system has so failed us, we the people must recompose ourselves, rediscover a meaning, language, and imagery dedicated enough to truth to
revive the memory that we exist and are entitled not merely to freedom but to full
possession of the world we are actually in. The author of the celebrated phrase "the
society of the spectacle," French Situationist Guy Debord, seemingly putting into
words one truth, may have spoken for Americanized ruling orders everywhere when

he stated, early on, that "in a world that is really upside down, the true is a moment of the false." Nothing could be more facile and more descriptive of the new dictatorship's method. This is precisely what we are meant to believe, the principle we are trained to accept. It describes the cold and dark orb that was the sun, exposing the collapsed stature of truth in theory and life and under it, a broad moral, political, scientific, even spiritual collapse. When reality is turned upside down, when what was is said to be is the opposite of what occurs—when actual events, people, and things are discredited—where can we turn but to something like the truth? Americans reject the notion there are any givens in life or on earth. The problem is that, when organized lying becomes the principle of power itself, it is the political system that makes truth into a moment of the false, upending everything given. Anything can be fabricated, remade, altered, and thrown away. The lie becomes more prolific in its evidence and consequences than any fact.

It is here that artists and poets have much to say, for while they may make things up, seek to escape, and may occasionally fall through the perilous mirror of beauty, they work within the indivisible web of our relations to ourselves, each other, and all that undeniably is. If the artist and poet are the first to "lie" in order to get at the truth, they do so to get at the world, not to remake and alter it according to the lie. The poets most of all inhabit and reside in the language, dedicating themselves to words and what they mean, how they mean, if they mean anything at all. Each person is born with a distinct vantage; the poets, sometimes even against their will, take up home there, at once in the language and serving it. They are, by some mysterious calling, engaged in sustaining language, pulled, even dragged out of the unknowable interior into a public realm they may rightly suspect. It is not necessarily truth they concern themselves with, but it is nonetheless truth that everyone gains in the restored and revitalized tongue. The American poet George Oppen introduced one of his books with an extraordinary phrase, drawn from the philosopher Martin Heidegger, citing "the arduous path of appearances." The philosopher demonstrably tumbled on this very path; the poets build, maintain, and walk it. They are forced, if you will, to engage in the first struggle, with language, not as children as we all are, but as adults.

If there is one thing a dictatorship fears, it is this unswerving dedication, not merely to meaning, which is threatening enough, but to a living language that is meaningful, reliable, and plural. Artists can concern themselves with imagery, sound, architecture, and movement, but it is the poets, and their inextricable relation to their vantages, worked through language, that confront the actual, and disturbingly malleable organization of the mind. The poet, in struggling with language, is made to think amidst the mind's most basic, essential parts. Language and speech are the heart of our capacity to understand; the poet shows that protection of such a thing is possible, building it up rather than merely giving in to organization as dictated by society, code, commerce, and most ambiguously of all, practicality.

The Cold War was, in numerous ways, possibly the first long-term and organized attack on the truth and the people's access to it in American history. While our history is filled with secrecy, half-truths, and even genocidal lies, never before has the society organized on such a scale, systematically, decade after decade, in every city, town, and countryside, around lying as a necessity. The Cold War may have ultimately constructed something truly horrific: a mass form uninterested in the truth, advancing and rewarding those who accept such a principle. The answer to such a thing can ultimately only be political, but first we must find where we are. The Nigerian novelist and storyteller Chinua Achebe, in *Home and Exile*, speaks of how colonialist regimes and their writers and artists produced stories that prepared the ground for seizure of land and power. Unfortunately, both disenfranchisement and enfranchisement begin with stories; it is necessary for every people to examine what exists and find their own, what he called "the process of 'restorying' peoples who had been knocked silent by the trauma of all kinds of dispossession." Is there any question peoples everywhere have been knocked silent by dispossession and trauma, built on a superstructure of falsehood? The New England poet Charles Olson offered up a comprehensively political response to his town paper in Gloucester, Mass, in 1965, as demolition and lies were deepening in every direction, calling for his township to "redeclare the ownership of all her public conditions." The problem for Americans is that the maneuvers Achebe refers to were not an endpoint, but pre-totalitarian; we are now much further along, and in need of a deeper, broader transformation to address this. A whole system has arisen to provide the people with meaning and stories that look like their own, that even have the correct skin color and gender, but that are, structurally and politically, shattering our relation to conditions, not merely through marching boots and violent collectivization, but through the undermining and loss of our distinct, and very precise, senses and experience of what is, what was, and what can be.

Fred Dewey 03

When politics and society have committed themselves to rule by lying, it is the artists and poets who remind us of the capacity to create meaning and discover truth, not as a group or society, but one at a time, each struggling inside language in their own way. It is true that poets and artists can be used, and even often offer themselves up for use and using. But as Abdellatif Laabi, the great Moroccan writer put it, emerging from a decade in prison, in his 1982 novel/memoir *Rue du Retour*— a book superior to many by European existentialists—in "this pasteboard theater," our "stage is now bare." The poet asks: "what does this mean in the war of attrition and tactics in which we have already lost a few battles?" "The powerful searchlight of the control tower did not melt the wax of your wings....Sleepwalking in daylight you carve out a path for yourself in the heart of the mass....you walk like any other of freedom's porters, oblivious to their precious cargo....You speak to those who can still hear the cry of man."

There are countless poets and artists for whom truth is a consequence. What matters, however, in the end, is the work, even if eked out of a prison cell on cigarette paper, as did the Syrian poet Faraj Bayrakdar (in a title forthcoming from Beyond Baroque, not excerpted here), or memorized, line by line, by a poet like Akhmatova, afraid to commit words even to scraps, or a filmmaker like Godard, struggling almost to exhaustion against the dictatorship of moving images and sounds (in a forthcoming title, excerpted here). As Laabi puts it, echoing the Russian poet Osip Mandelstam, "This land, just two steps away. How will you rediscover it with your own eyes, ears, hands?" In contrast to the open brutalities of modern-day political prisons, often paid for by us, the trauma and dispossession perfected by the American model penetrate the soul deviously, hidden, as total movement from within and without. Only work that does not serve a function, that does not aspire merely to putting food on the table or doing what the rest of society is doing, can answer it. This requires going deep, and mercilessly, into the vantage one has been given. This is the one thing the poet—whatever their stated political beliefs—does that no one else can equal. It is this, when in the company of others, that brings us back to preservation of some kind of fact and objectivity, to that foundation of our freedom that is the struggle with language.

Because of one's senses, one's vantage turns simultaneously inward and outward. The two realms may feel different, but they are only distinct; they exist together in the world. Muriel Rukeyser once wrote that "nothing was true in the sense I wanted it to be true." Her answer? To speak of actual people, in one case a scientist and poet Willard Gibbs, who "binds himself to know the public life of systems." "Look through the wounds of law/ at the composite face of the world," she declared. In 1946, as his involvement with Trumanite party politics and government was souring (partly the subject of another forthcoming book, by Ammiel Alcalay), Olson framed our dilemma: "What have you to help you hold in a single thought reality and justice?" A poet spends difficult hours trying to figure out what it is they think, feel, see, hear, know, touch, and must research, and whether these do or do not relate to the world. Language may pour out, images may tumble together in a pile, but in the end, it is in the world that these must find their home. This delicate persistence is only more significant and courageous when its path is answered, as today, by a world where torture has become the principle of government itself.

The poet and artist understand better than anyone that things are true or not regardless of the numbers that support or reject them. This already tells us a little. They do something that, in a time of lies, no solely political person, or witting or unwitting social climber, can. They create lasting works that, whether they are truthful, metaphoric, or outright fabrications, uphold the life of truth, in meaningfulness and persistence, as a living relation to the difficult world without and opaque realm within. They stitch together a fabric of strands capable of holding truth aloft, there for us to see it *can* be held up and not hide, flee, or dictate. Politics has never been on good terms with truth; indeed, it seems to be opposed to it in its very essence. When it is pursued by and on behalf of the people, however, politics is concerned with the architecture of things, building a space and time for what matters and is significant. When such a politics has been crushed and exterminated, as it has today, it is the artists and poets who keep it alive and give truth a context and web in which to regain its footing. As the Spanish writer Jordi Pujol Nadal wrote recently in a Spanish rock and roll magazine, on reading the work of Venice Beat Philomene Long (featured here), "You cannot be indifferent." It is possible, in fact, that "one phrase can save you."

One such phrase, caught by the artist Christoph Draeger and presented here, appeared on a Mexico City billboard during the people's anti-fraud protests of summer 2006. It was from the historian, writer, and rights activist Elena Poniatowska: "How to build a great country? By saying the truth." Can one imagine such a phrase any more in the United States? The difficulty, of course, is that the things destroying us are as much a part of truth as what might save us, whether we choose to respect them and think about them or not. As such, up against a world movement of the lie, we must work to build something deeper and more durable than the protections offered by mere human rights and struggles to protect a particular person or group. What would a Solzhenitsyn, for example, have to say about political conditions in America, now? Who favors or for that matter remembers, here, his relentless, detailed focus on historical crimes and their effect on an entire society, top to bottom? Would an American novelist dare venture into such terrain? Truth deserves such attention and care. As Olson understood, it demands research and self-education, digging into the foundations of our life to explore, rethink, and work things from a generous instinct for political equality in all domains. Truth may come to us in the shape of myth, the shape of history, in fable or fact, but it needs to be spoken and addressed to all. No society based on absence of truth can be happy or endure, precisely because truth remains everywhere. The constant organizing motion of the lie assuages, relieves, even stimulates us against it, but leaves only ruins, with their shards, edges, plunging and broken matter, death, confusion, and homelessness. It was the Nazis, learning from both the Americans and Stalin, who elevated the use of ruination to a supreme, Western art form; we have barely begun to understand how far this has now gone.

The danger the American society of the lie poses to its people and the world must be understood by Americans. What is broken and collapsed is an elemental activity. If so much is ruined, what theory, poem, or series of images can possibly answer this over-arching propaganda, brutality, and worst of all, pragmatism that is so relentlessly destroying everything? The apparently politically fruitless activity of artists and poets is not at all fruitless. The ruination of the senses, of the heart and mind, may turn out to have been the American system's method, going back certainly to the beginning of the 20th century, and possibly all the way back to the end of Reconstruction. The achievement of this disordering of the senses is reaching an unbearable and fatal degree. We need a massive reconstruction, re-awakening, rebuilding, re-rooting, and re-constitution. But it is at the most basic level of our senses and faculties that this begins. It is there that art and poetry provide us with something irreplaceable. It is there that recovering the people's land and power, our democracy and republic, practices its first, faltering, unsteady steps.

LETTER TO JACK SPICER

Dear Jack,

Every time I go into a bookstore, I still check under "S" to see if, by any chance, the Martians—or anyone else for that matter—might have brought in something new from you. I'll never forget the night *The Collected Books* arrived—it was at that little shop on Sheridan Square. I could check but I think it's either a cell phone place now or the entrance to a health club that takes up the whole block. Of course I already had all the White Rabbit stuff and the various pirated editions, but this was different, with the embossed black, white, and red cover, and Robin's essay that I stayed up most of the night reading. I don't even know if you would have approved of the whole thing. That was in 1975.

There's so much I want to tell you, Jack—it's like my whole life can be hinged to that moment, holding the book that night, with you already dead ten years, thinking about the befores and afters, the directions taken and not taken. In 1975, when I was working at Jacques Auto Body in the Mission and Custom Body near Howard Street, I went to a few of the bars in North Beach that you used to hang out in. Years later, when I went back to San Francisco in the capacity of an officially recognized poet, I got to know an old friend of yours, Fran Herndon, and she showed me the collage of Willie Mays that she had done with a clipping from, I think, *Sports Illustrated*. The Say Hey Kid, after whom I renamed myself Willie one summer in grade school when I got sick and tired of having to go through the agony of correctly pronouncing my name for people and realized I could tell new people I met a new name and no one would be the wiser.

Not much has changed—of course, that's not exactly true, I mean, the Giants don't play in Candlestick anymore and the Red Sox have actually won a World Series. What I really mean is that when you spoke in Berkeley on July 14th, 1965, about not taking the loyalty oath back in 1950, you said: "The word McCarthy is a nice word to use, but it wasn't just McCarthy. It was the whole thing—the Korean War and everything else." The Korean War.

Here's a poem I thought you should read, it's called "The Long March":

North from Pusan,
trailing nooses of dust,
we dumbly followed
leaders whose careers
hung on victory.

The road might
have been the Appian Way
except for the
starving children lining it.
We gave what we could

to hold back the grave,
but in Pusan the dead-truck
snuffled through frozen dawns
retrieving bones in thin sacks,
kids who would never beg again.

When we bivouacked
near Pyongtaek, a soldier
fished a bent brown stick
from a puddle. It was
the arm of someone's child.

Not far away, the General
camps with his press corps.
Any victory will be his.
For us, there is only
the long march to Viet Nam.

Who knows, given the way the last century's gone, maybe in retrospect things have actually been getting better. The poem was written, I think, some time in the 1960s, by a guy named William Childress, a little younger than you, though older now that you're dead. He was born in Oklahoma and grew up in a family of sharecroppers and migrant cotton pickers. He joined the army in 1951, at the age of eighteen, and served in Korea as a demolitions expert and secret courier. The poem reminds me a lot of the question that Sister Mary Norbert Korte asked you that same day in Berkeley, after your talk, when the discussion veered towards the political effects of poetry, and names like Brecht, Mayakovsky, and Shelley were brought up. When Sister Mary said: "Perhaps you don't consider this poetry, but what about the labor songs of the thirties," you said it was "a damn good question," and came back singing "Pie in the Sky" by Joe Hill. I can't remember how I got a hold of her books, but I do remember that she quoted you, Charles Olson, Robert Duncan, David Meltzer, Lew Welch, the *Book of Job*, and a bunch of other things in *Hymn to the Gentle Sun*. She wrote *Beginning of Lines* as a response to Kenneth Patchen's *Journal of Albion Moonlight*, a book very few people read anymore. Looking back on it, I'd have to say her poetry was like a secret that I only shared with a few close friends.

There seems to be a lot of talk these days, what with new wars going on, about how poets "should" write or speak. Various commissars are prescribing and proscribing, some in favor of "ambiguity," "complexity," and "skepticism," and others in favor of some variation of "plain speech" or "direct statement." Like so much of what passes for debate here, much of the discussion gets displaced, with people fluctuating wildly from almost obscene diatribe and personal insult to polite gentility. Often, as in my own case, the person or body of work largely responsible for opening up the issues is simply not referred to, or only obliquely. Kind of like walking into a room of people you think you know and no one even gestures in your direction, like you're invisible. Given your relationship to ghosts, none of this should surprise you. It does make me wonder, though, whether you're better off dead. Look, there's one last thing that I can't really explain to you—you'll just have to try and figure it out for yourself, wherever you are: pennant races aren't really pennant races anymore. Although you're almost always on my mind when I'm writing, I'm not sure if I'll address any more letters directly to you.

yours,

Willie

poetry
is
news

LUMINOUS SOLIDARITY

A 40-watt lamp is burning in my room.
A captive inside its pale circle,
I pass my evenings: reading
and writing, daubs and scratchings,
an entire volume of discarded
foolscap. And Trikoupi Street
gradually grows quiet—only around two or three
the occasional roar of a motor
forces a passage. I count again and again,
the lights still on in the tenements
around, certain that someone else
finds comfort in counting
mine. Yet I must hasten,
write what I can, whatever I've time for,
before it goes out, the final light
that keeps me awake.

—translated from the Greek by Yiannis Goumas

There are no answers.
There are a few poems.

THE SCARAB

…and the truth is, I no longer care
what I think, or whether it is true
or not, germane to any outer thing
or not. I am willing to write it,
if the poem will accept it. I serve
no lesser lord; I serve the poem.

And the poem holds a secret it waits
patiently to share. Even with me.

The real world, they say, the real world.
But mind, hand, and pen are one.
Iridescent insect, scarab confounding taxonomy—
it, and the web which holds it, struggling:
they are one. All serves the poem.

PERSISTENCE OF WATER

Poetry's not held in vessels of mud.
I said: I'll stop writing, for a couple of years,
and let poetry speak through other mouths.
I'll forget it. I will not be called a poet.
Now I'll become a teacher, a laborer, a clerk.
I will not listen to that inner anthill,
the din of sheets snapped by the wind.
But poetry finds its way,
like water filtering through
a plaster wall.
So to begin once again,
as from fear, to choke
the noise of the leaves.
Poetry doesn't spill like wine;
it's not bartered for with thirty coins of silver;
its doesn't even hide like talents in the ground.
Poetry ruptures your mouth.

—translated from the Spanish by Anthony Seidman

From I, ZOOLOGICAL

I

At my birth they filled me with hot coals
and I was the night boiling over.
My eyes became pregnant with fire
and among foreign fires I consumed myself to the point of vertigo.
I was a loyal dweller of paradise, and I uttered
coal-singed poems in sleepwalking languages
that illumined the desert at night.
Now I live hidden and exiled in the land because I know
true poems are great blazes
and here
embers burn in the dazzling tracks of my species.

—translated from the Spanish by Anthony Seidman

ELECTRIC FLESH

discontinuous memories of the besieged current

If it were an animal, it would be a baboon, a hirsute rage, with a gnarled fury ready to go slack at the least caress, but it isn't an animal, it's only a date—date or disaster, same difference, same water brought to various degrees of boiling or ignorance, it's what unties tongues when they thicken, it's what rouses rats when they come aboard, it's the 7th of August 1881, the year when President Garfield is shot, when the leading dinosaurs (*brontosaurus amplus*) are christened, when the great Pop Smith plays for the Buffalo Bisons, and in fact it takes place in Buffalo (United States), not far from Niagara Falls (in Indian: *Onguiaahra*, "straits"), it is near 11 p.m. and George L. Smith, 31 years old, dockworker by trade & alcoholic in fact, following-up a not very bright bet with his brother Vince, tries to couple with the Brush Electric Light Company generator, located on Ganson Street.

The aforementioned generator however doesn't flaunt particularly exciting curves: it's a stupefied pachyderm, kneeling in its own power, overhauled in a rush and as a result quite prone to outages.

George advances, titillated by the regular purring of the generator which is dreaming about curdling all his molecules. The thing gapes, parts silky and rusty skirts, arches its back. The energy emitted is such that any resistance immediately makes it increase. It's a remarkable moment: when desire treats ridicule disdainfully so as to return to its forbidden roots, where to bend is to become an arc, no matter the arrows, no matter the target, blood becomes bone, bone bends, *tschaaak!* Hardly has George placed his two callous-set paws on the zinc friction plates (first the right—tinglings—then the left—*zrrip! ting!*, then his entire mental & emotional system is absorbed and dissolved, his balls shrink like knucklebones in a geezer's fist, the puddled cry that he is about to retch out dries at the rim of his nostrils, the temperature of his bladder climbs in a half second to 95 degrees, his vision inverts, there, all his memories are reduced to the size of the head of a pin which sinks without jolts and without hesitation into the deliquescent marrow of his urges—the poorly sequenced scrapbook of his life explodes fanlike and pollinates his last moments, he rethinks, resees, reneges, at once extremely volatile and overcome by gravity once and for all, *schomp! schomp! schomp!* leaden images strike his hide—in the disorder: the surprised face of his mother, a glove between thighs, the taste of maple sap while staying in Montreal, a barber's flickering sign in the early hours of

September when he came back *fully intoxicated* after a prolonged immersion in the land of venal pleasures, the nail torn off when he lifted a 99 lb. crate, all that, all those things not worth recording but worthy only of being forgotten are instantaneously mixed ground tamped down then melted into a hard point, tempered by the moment of death, simultaneously galvanized and annihilated. The George L. Smith constellation has just entered its nothingness phase. *Paralysis of the nerves of respiration*, concludes coroner Joseph Fowler the next day, performing the autopsy at the authority's request. The heart has stopped as suddenly as a union activist under the convincing blow of the billy club. There apparently wasn't any "pain"—

> *(and that the pain must be rather incredible to not be apparent, that the body does its utmost to give no evidence of it, muscular or otherwise, that's what starts one thinking, and which makes of this thought an even more abominable pain.)*

The designated Smith has just inaugurated the litany of the Oft Toasted of Pan-Electric History. Without knowing, he attains the rank of pioneer of the new American frontier, that which will tame continuous current and imprison the Wild West of bodies in a reservation under voltametrical surveillance.

Here's where the Great Extractor intervenes…

ADVERTISEMENT:
"Tremble, oh tender gums, and you mediocre molars, for your patron saint has just walked into the patent Shop. The constructor of crowns, the encruster of fillings sees his reign begin."

He's a dentist, called Alfred Porter Southwick, and when at breakfast he falls upon coroner Fowler's report, when he savors its barbecue-prose ("exceedingly rare fact, the brains were cooked"), he senses that his fate of being a stump puller is about to undergo an unexpected revolution. Southwick, thus thus thus, declares out of the blue that electricity, toyed with at low voltage, could:

1) *replace Anesthetic during medical operations;*
2) *become a form of Euthanasia for all unwanted stray animals falling under the responsibility of the city.*

Affixing his silver forceps onto the twin foreheads of his two newborn girls, savage Euthanasia and bitch Anesthesia, the former dentist becomes *de facto* the wicked stepmother of the undesirables, of beasts first, then of men. He organizes a crusade the way others launch a subscription, and treats himself to the help of two wicked fairies,

Dr. George E. Fell, zealous electrotherapist, inventor of the "Fell Motor" (a pulmonary reanimator which we don't have anything to do with here, and certainly not elsewhere), and Colonel Rockwell, president of the Buffalo Society of the Prevention of Cruelty to Animals. These three men, which even a sexual deviance would be enough to bring together, throw themselves into a series of experiments on stray dogs and cats which could no longer decently continue to be decently drowned in the river. An alcoholic dockworker understood how to properly bow out—if one didn't dwell too long on the burns on the palms and the gray matter brought to a white heat—so it must be possible in the same way to eliminate all four-legged criminals from the street.

Agreement of tenses and empathy of places: the opponents of capital punishment, hostile to the gibbet and anxious to finally give pain a reasonable Richter scale, the defenders of vertical dignity raise their voices, hoist them, even, up to the skies & to the judges' doorsteps. A current of opinion starts to quiver through the great democratic soup: hangings, often (and because) slapdash, start giving off with the help of press and attorney a medieval whiff which immediately perfumes the pathetic concept of pathetic progress. Just as one right can cut across another only if each finds pleasure and interest in that bisection, so a certain MacMillan, sidekick to Southwick, advances the hypothesis according to which a painless death will nail shut the capital-punishment-abolishers' traps. MacMillan, whose wife just perished, drowned in a slurry pit, MacMillan whom his contemporaries describe as a "spat out seed coming back to haunt the idea of the fruit which released it"—which was said of him quite long into his adult life—consults Governor David Bennett Hill, who quickly makes a proposal to the Legislature aiming to replace the gallows with electricity. A commission is set:

The Death Commission*

Whose purpose is, let's cite & savor, "to study and to bring to public consciousness the most humane and most effective method there is to successfully complete the execution of the death sentence."

Southwick, of course, indispensable abscess in the humanitarian maw, is named as primary expert with two other members, two bold barking heavies by the names of Matthew Hale and Elbridge T. Gerry. A man of law doubling as a brilliant orator,

---

* DC, as in Direct Current, Divine Comedy, Double Collision, Dominate Carnally, Dismembered Character, Danse Coupable…Don't Come!

Hale will know how to sort out legal difficulties. Gerry is the founder of the American Society for the Prevention of Cruelty to Animals and Children (but not cadavers). A 95-page report inventorying all past and present forms of extermination is written up—forced labor unfortunately doesn't appear therein, nor does sexual abstinence or electioneering. A 5-point questionnaire, mentioning electrocution, is addressed to hundreds of experts from every sex (as long as they're male). Responses rush in, numerous, nearly two hundred. A certain Dr. Brill, originally of New York City, assesses that since lightning doesn't kill at every strike, it is useless to expect anything from electricity; J. Henry Furman, of Tarrytown, proposes a metallic chair whose legs rest in a zinc solution; Alfred Carroll, of New Brighton, is also inclined in favor of electricity, because according to him the gallows no longer have any dissuasive power, they even have a certain prestige, a folkloric aura which urges the criminal to inscribe himself into the grim legend, it's a platform, a stage, *a fucking podium!* Professor Elihu Thompson estimates the cost of a lethal battery at two hundred dollars maximum and commits to fabricate/mass-produce them.

Thomas Alva Edison is content with sending a letter to Southwick on the 8th of November 1887 to remind him that he is opposed to capital punishment and a believer in reincarnation. But on the 9th of the following December, Edison drafts a second letter, in which he writes: `"The most suitable apparatus for the purpose is that class of dynamo-electric machinery which employs alternating currents, manufactured principally in this country by George Westinghouse."` Edison, the apostle of the continuous, immediately proposes the alternative, the spearhead of his direct competitor, George Westinghouse, because he understands that by associating discontinuous current and capital punishment, he is damaging his rival: who would dare invite into his house the executioner's lights? And here's Edison pushing his quite plump luck into a hardly clearer shadow and managing to acquire an alternating current generator, under the very nose of his hated rival. He throws himself body & bucks into a series of savage experiments, grills dogs, cats, horses, elephants, before presenting to the Death Commission his model *made in holy wood*, the 1st Electric Chair, the very one which will roast the murderer William Kemmler on the 6th of August 1890 at the Auburn prison.

aborted escapology attempt

Another date, other facts, another life—another name, also: Howard Hordinary.

It is Saturday the 14th of August 1996. It is exactly 7:28 p.m., *tixit* the living room wall clock. The adventures of Southwick & Co, the baboons massacred on the assembly line, the battle of currents, the first human barbecues in Auburn or Sing-Sing Prison, Howard knows all this, and for good reason, he is an executioner, an electric executioner, well almost since here he is, unemployed, once more, lack of clients, the State of Pennsylvania just having opted for lethal injection. Out of work, Howard returns to his first love, the mind-numbing worship of Harry Houdini—our man, following Gary Gilmore's lead, is persuaded he is the unlikely grandson of the celebrated magician. This belief, like digestion complicated by drowsiness, is the cause of surprising mental ferment. Thus, Howard has long believed that his ghostly granny is none other than Charmian London, the wife of Jack London with whom Houdini had messed around, but through more or less orthodox research he has come to wonder if his grandmother isn't instead the enigmatic *SZUSZU*, the Electric Girl who shared the billing with Jumbo and the Cannon-Man. He'll have to talk to his mother, Emily, about it next time he brings her cookies at the hospice. In the meantime, he lets his cigarette fall into the circle of coffee forming a mirror at the bottom of his mug, throws a glance out the window at the neighbor's garden, the dog sleeps in front of his kennel, its skeleton well sheltered under his fleabitten hide, a cat crosses the alley as if passing beneath barbed wire. Howard almost didn't sleep at all last night.

After having carefully avoided his wife Bess at the end of the kitchen and in the area around the living room, a Bess who does her best to limp to remind her husband that a pair of new shoes wouldn't be too reckless an offering, Howard shuts himself first in his study, upstairs.

The room offers to the dust all sorts of runways on which various transitory objects leave their outlines from one day to the next (example: the imprint of scissors biting into the circumference of a quarter). A grimy PC occupies the center of the work table and hardly whimpers, the space bar worried. The computer screen throws back at him to begin with an etching of blurred lines, his own, and he must increase the brightness to the maximum for this muddy reflection to be succeeded by the block of instructions that he hasn't ceased embellishing for the last three weeks: THE DESIGN OF AN ELECTROCUTION SYSTEM INVOLVES THE CONSIDERATION OF A FEW, BUT VERY SIGNIFICANT, REQUIREMENTS. VOLTAGE, CURRENT, CONNECTIONS, DURATION AND NUMBER OF CURRENT APPLICATIONS (JOLTS). His fingers tiptap a few buttons while his eyes ascend

slowly toward the photo of a girl in a swimsuit, subtitled *SZUSZU* THE ELEC-
TRIC BITCH (1887-1909), and dedicated in soft pencil to Harry Houdini—
SZUSZU who seems to contemplate him from behind a windowpane frosted by
boredom, her two arms raised in a flared V, each of her ten fingers connected by tin-
gling cobwebs (30 volts certainly) to two generators trademarked **Godhison Inc.**
Under the stiff swimsuit, breasts and pubis thrust out, and even the seal of the navel,
miniscule switch. In the background, a little to the left, one makes out the smudged
silhouette of a sidekick decked out in a baboon mask: Houdini?

The screen of the computer excretes onto its surface a livid pool which knots
into a loop before rushing to the upper right corner of the monitor. Without realizing it Howard has turned the machine off. Without realizing it, he sat up straight
and brought his big nose close to the paned face of *SZUSZU*, his tongue came out
between his teeth, while below, against the frame of the monitor, the fabric of his
pants strains over the contained arc of his erection. The lips of the woman seem to
move away from one another, a hesitant mollusk parts saliva forming a bubble, a—

Hoooooward!

Too bad.

Bess is calling him.

She must have found, hidden under a corner of carpet, the magazine that Sam
Turnpike yielded to him the other night at the *Bright Angel Bar* in exchange for a
mega-round of drinks. Sam is his only friend, even if the only thing that interests
Sam is to set Howard onto doubtful paths, fornication for three or four, with fleet-
ing women, girls with whom he experiments on with all sorts of gadgets, you got no
idea, since you haven't worn one you can't imagine. Vaguely disgusted, Howard has
nonetheless ended by giving in. He promised Sam to come join one of these pathetic
orgies some evening, all the more reason since his electric talents, he has been made
to understand, are not without use. In the meantime, Howard looks in Sam's magazine for indications, for grounds for self-indulgence: those shared and spreading slits
those shiny gaping asses those breasts closed in a vice on the tips those pushed in
objects those too long hands those smiles daubed red and especially those eyes
which, mysteriously, don't follow you when the magazine slides to the left or to the
right according to whether the right knee or the left knee hiccoughs while he yes
beats yes off yes, all those attributes crammed between the glossy covers of the magazine must—imperatively!—be envisioned only from a servo-mechanical angle, yes
yes yes, they are tools in a toolbox, nuts, screws, nails and rivets, greased pistons, and

by supposing that the body is properly speaking this machinery which society covets, by supposing that by lubricating/plugging in/inserting one always ends up obtaining less rebellious surfaces softer angles and more subtle articulations, so there is in this certainly material to invent something else, and since Howard Hordinary has no other desire here below than the worship of evasion and the perfecting of a certain electrical device (which is waiting for him, on the mezzanine, where he will go soon, very soon), since to Bess he refuses even the least soothing touch, why ever not, why not, not, do, here, there, ha-uh, a few, uh, adjustments, like that, without a level, ah, or a chalk-line, oh, de-li-ca-te-ly, guesswork of the fle-uh-esh, yes, in the wood's knot the iron-hard fiber, MARVELOUS, see how the girl in the centerfold looks like she can be mistaken misshapen misread for *SZUSZU*, with a felt pen he closes her eyelids and puts his giant's index finger on her dwarf's pubis, but of course nothing happens, flop-flop, the ink eventually stains the whorls of his pulp, and when he brings the finger to his tongue the taste he reaps isn't worth, at the outside, a glass of bourbon even cut with water. He cuts the current.

It isn't the magazine Bess has exhumed, but one more invoice: electric components, soldering lamp, circuit breaker casing, three-phase wiring...*Shit!* Howard sends back to limbo the portrait of his grandmother/courtesan and leaves his study. He passes before Bess without even favoring her with an ox-like wink and, body upset & mind warped, grabs his cluster of keys and goes down to the mezzanine, there where nearly eleven years of sedimented illusions are going moldy: posters illuminated with the red of abbatoirs, boxes full of cards, scaled rings, dried bouquets, Gordian knots, volumes tattooed with gilded riddles—the name of Houdini repeated in all sense of publicity and bluff, extolled at the head of all the leaflets—all the flashy rubbish of the great Houdini, peritonised some seventy years earlier: ropes, chains, above all handcuffs—The Maltby Dead Lock Shackles, The Extraordinary Bean Giant Handcuffs, The Regulation Double Lock Tower Leg-Irons, The Double Lock Tower Ratchet, The Navy Handcuff Slave Iron, The Nova Scotia Leg-Iron, & The Parish Thumb-Screws & The Pinkerton Handcuff—

Enough!

Enough!

ENOUGH!

—*translated from the French by Brian Evenson*

GOING TO THE DOGS

When dogs bark, I taste October.
I fall into disrepair.
I crave a new green sweater.
I miss my husbands.
I miss my dolly.
I gulp down a lot of dolls.

When dogs bark, I drink up the Brunello.
Also the Pinot Noir and the Chianti.
I get ravenous for French Fries.
I want to leave *immediatment* for Paris.
I change my name to Emma Bovary.
I change my name to Scarlett O'Hara.
My name changes itself to Carrie.

When dogs bark, the road shimmers in an evil way.
The sentences go missing.
The dictionary smokes meaning into nothing.
I stare at the works of Hiroshige.
I see myself in a kimono and obi.
I am totally obified.

When dogs bark, Baba–Yaga swoops over the house.
The radio gets a panic attack.
The refrigerator agitates for freedom.
The orchard gets a headache.
The peach tree shudders with omens.
The dark's a coven of rattles and claws.
The cat sings.
I don't have a cat.

Barking dogs!

The moon is a white poppy!
The moon is a white guppy!
The moon is a white puppy!

Barking dogs!
I translate texts into the lingo of parakeets!
I transubstantiate multiplication tables into porno!
I tear open windows and doors to lightning and madness!

Barking ! Barking! Barking !

GOOD NIGHT STORY

Once upon a time there was a cat named Housey and it was a house cat. The cat was chased by a dog all the time and it drove the owners crazy. The dog would try to eat the cat. And there was a bird and the cat would try to eat the bird and the bird tried to eat a spider and the spider tried to eat a mosquito and the mosquito tried to eat a flea. Now the owners were allergic to cats and didn't see the spider...but it was a black widow and they thought it was a tarantula. And the owners of the pets were named...Jake and his step brother... Jakey. And their cousin... Paul and his sister... Jessica and her little sister... Charlene! And there was this door and it could talk! And every time someone opened it it would say, "Hellooo Hellooo Hellooo" (think Count Olaf). And so there was this cat...well you know the people had so many pets that they had to get rid of almost all of them. All except a little tiny puppy. And the mommy and the daddy because they needed to take care of their puppy. So the little tiny golden retriever puppy was swinging on a swing and jumped off and was flying to the moon! And he landed there and met an angel named... Jessica and one named... Michelle and one named... *She burps*...Burpy! Because it burped a lot, so I named it Burpy. And there was a fairy and rainbow colored guards and it was a peaceful planet named... Joke-a-Lot, because everybody always told jokes. And so the little puppy told a joke and everyone couldn't stop laughing. They laughed for a whole hour! ...actually two hours. And there was a friendly bear. And you know what? It ate the puppy. But it's okay because it just swallowed the puppy, it didn't chew and so it threw the puppy back up and the puppy was covered in honey. And so it ran home and they lived happily ever after. Good Night ~ The End.

EXACTITUDE

Not didactic addition, or superimposed forensics hoisted upon a psychic limestone slab, but exactitude, as a state, over and above the blizzard of static. A static made up of integers, and forms of integers, empowered across its field by exoteric procreation.

Fact at the level of popular cerebral exhibit, can never organically respirate as poetic neural balance. The latter experiences itself as auric exploration, which inevitably accrues from auric harmonics. Again, right balance. So sums at this level are akin to Daumal's savor, where essences intermingle, where the facts of the world then partake of the zone of tintinnabulation.

THE GHOST SURVIVOR

Body by drosera
by pure calliope as referent
as invaded mausoleum

the body then existing
as standing cinder under threat
condensed
brought back to the soil
as a sub-abandoned heresy
being a blue in-carnivorous thought arrangement
under an orange-white dust
next to a blank & verdigris spinning house

& this spinning house
brazen with tarantulas & probing
with its sun posts imploding
with its Macaws & adders as regressive sub-orders

the body in this haze
an apparitional ballast
a half form quaking
flowing through faceless compost arcana

calling out from jeopardous blindings
from disrupted falcons & armies
like salt without form
like general anthracite gone missing

ON A PHRASE FROM PENTHEUS THE CRETAN

All (1. lethal word in a 'time of particulars' 2. employed
in an attempt to mask distinctions 2a. lofted like a net 2b.
even the sound of the word lingers as an inclusive breath,
the final breath, that is, before exhaustion 3. to harbor particulars 3a. to shelter & never disclose at first peek 3b. an
utterance which forsakes multiplicity) **Cretans** (1. the un-
discovered script, 'Linear X,' is flushed from History 2. the
pictogram obscures the 'thing' it stands for 3. obsession
for the dolphin's gaze on an amphora as it speaks of an innocence which nullifies 4. pirates before the cusp of the
Christian millennia 5. the bronze on the lions in downtown Heraklion blinks, scatters light fervently 6. to inhabit
the remnants of 'a hundred cities' 6a. what temple arises
from buried pride? 7. adoration for the 'broad-browed'
princess, Europa, the graceful supplicant) **Are** (1. this author
refuses to posture any shade of Being) **Liars** (1. charlatans
of reality 2. a case of becoming the word one uses 3. being
a matter of breath, vision, & spectacle 4. the ghosts in the
window 5. those who sleep during the day & wail away
at night unknown to themselves but with the purest of knowledge)

THE FENCE

At a certain moment
after having left the house
you thought that you had forgotten something
an object
something unknown
and that it was necessary to turn back

a certain time
while in the middle of childish games and joy
a word took you by surprise
and you turned your eyes elsewhere in search of it

then with undeniable fear
a voice surprised you while you spoke
another one
simply another
and when the night offered itself to you
vast and traversable
you became aware how
between the dust and the city
poetry was building us a fence

—translated from the Spanish by Anthony Seidman

from SPINNING POLYHEDRAL MIRROR (Part 1)

1.
Though our breakup made me swallow fifty sleeping pills
She gives me fifty-one reasons to have insomnia

2.
When love no longer penetrates to the bone
The meat of your body starts eating meat for meat's sake

3.
Suddenly we see each other
Already we are on the same road

4.
Artists often lean their bodies
Over the edge of two extremes
From their mouths come finely crafted shouts for help

5.
Reader, if you happen to be a doctor
How will you face a writer using onset of mania
To write the human body?

6.
????

7.
His hands were blackened from groping in darkness
Since then the color black has not left his pen

8.
While I lie beneath my quilt in an alien land
Honeybees get insomnia from the native-language embroidery

9.
Each time the road in a novel
Flashes the image of a country girl
I always feel myself shoulder a hoe

10.
If the soil temperature of the land I love would rise half a degree
Go ahead and bury me alive

11.
Dreams are the only forest that mankind cannot clearcut

12.
In the bed of my coffin I will continue my insomnia

13.
Use a backhoe on the horizon to dig the sun up early

14.
I want to operate recklessly
I'm not a genius
I'm a 20th Century machine
And I like playing with electricity

15.
Suicide is the only door
That gets locked from the other side
Using the human body as a key

16.
My nearsightedness must wear tears to see life clearly

17.
You have to grow into a weapon
To lie in the grass and not be bitten by bugs

18.
Life in the end is a piece of carved wood
That once was grown by green leaves

19.
Another name for pollution is lack of personality
People who lack personality cause pollution

20.
You ask about pets?
In the 22nd Century
I'm going to keep a cageful of fighter planes

21.
My blood cries to your blood
Let's not circulate in a battlefield

22.
Over the holidays
May I be led like a balloon in your hand
A balloon filled with hope blown in by your mouth

23.
Tomorrow
I will rest in a museum by fixing up a few hours of war
Tomorrow
Smuggling peace to other planets I will not accept U.S. dollars

24.
I don't want to ride a sickbed into the 21st Century
But the 21st Century rides into my body on a sickbed of its own

25.
With all the dark clouds of the world as my witness
I was born to hold my own umbrella

26.
Each time I turn my head
I stretch my collar out of shape
Because my home and I ran away from home together

27.
In the forest of New York, I chase a beast called "Loneliness"
I don't think being lonely makes its fur any less warm

28.
To live like a stone, many conditions must be met
Besides texture, color, temperature, and shape
You have to know more of the earth's historical secrets
Than mankind does, yet not speak of them

29.
No matter how young you are
Within your mind, you have to take care of the senior citizen named "Thought"

30.
A wristwatch is the cruelest device for torturing time

31.
If you want to borrow more sorrow from humanity you have to stand in line
But whom have the world's saddest sorrows been lent to?
Only the evader of debt knows for sure

32.
The whole world strikes a harmonica-playing pose
As it consumes the American music within a hamburger

33.
If I were a rat
I would undermine the world's walls
And sing how underground life goes in all directions

34.
Any kind of society can be the workout room for my inspiration
Until I buff myself into an exercise machine

35.
"Who winds the earth's mainspring?"
I wonder each day
As I turn the doorknob

36.
In crowded environments, people temper each other into steel
But too much steel causes steel prices to fall

37.
Many people crowd along the mass-production line of life
Because repetition is the nest of the weak

38.
After plunging into themselves
Many people find they cannot swim

39.
In the dynastic succession of daily necessities
Common folk always vote to be common

40.
Preserve the animals!
Preserve the stock market's herd of industrial horses
That often throw riders to the ground

41.
In places where my countrymen have wept for a long time
They begin to make salt

42.
Any one person in this world is superfluous
But according to the laws of economics
Only surplus money can be invested

43.
On vacation away from the city
A rhino took cover in the Africa of my heart
But rifles of conventionality reminded me
How keenly they smell the value of aphrodisiac horns

44.
Wind blows fish-songs into the city
I smell a salt tang from beyond the net

45.
I like freedom
But I feel that a cage is too bulky to wear

46.
Humanity is the aftermath of humanity

47.
A nest is life imposed upon a tree by birds

48.
A head-on wind is combing my hair
For beauty's sake
I do not look back

49.
Anyplace I go, I do the simplest manual work
Tearing apart bird cages
In front of any mirror I repeat the most primitive motions
Preening my feathers

50.
An event that makes the collective face turn red
Only happens in back alleys of a nation's consciousness

51.
Underground literature comes from roots adrift within the soil

52.
Inter-party conflict has to elevate the reason for a gang fight
To national or racial status
Because that is where the convalescents get the best treatment

53.
Walking along
If you don't kick something, you start to look effete
He has the word "door" embroidered on his trouser leg
The door to a nation

54.
Lovely germs spread across your face
Waiting to multiply into a smile
Ah, my daughter
Such eternal germs
Guarantee that my son-in-law will be an outstanding patient

55.
That is a forest where furniture easily grows
In it lives my house

56.
Book after book soars by up above
The sky that has leafed through countless wings
After reading the joy of a nest
Hatches pure blue expanses in people's eyes

57.
Parents want to nurture every brick in the house
Into a memorial plaque

58.
The broken bridge in the scenic painting on the wall
Proves that history since then had to swim across the water

59.
In this world
Only birds' nests in scenic photographs are left with a sense of security
I go farther and hide within unexposed film

60.
Sharp edges of ice are my feathers
As long as spring doesn't come
I can glide with ease back to my grave

61.
Music stirs the dancing crowd
Like a spoon stirring sugar in coffee
To take care of my inner dance floor
I gulp the spoon right down

62.
Mankind is planet earth's prime commodity
Unfortunately, the chances for export are exceedingly small

63.
Plants all go from flower to fruit
Only humans can stop at the flower

64.
Now that life has planted sunlight in my body
On the tips of these rays, I want to form gloomy fruits

I refuse to repeat sunlight on top of sunlight

65.
The patient's pet-loving complex is beyond treatment
He has the capacity to accept the running dogs of all dictators

66.
Two pieces of cloth cut from a flag
Patch my worn shirt at the elbows
I feel my sleeves being lifted by a carefree-beggar breeze

67.
Hearing the cough of bread that has grown moldy
Wheat sprouts slow down the pace of their growing

68.
On the back side of the world map is a blank space
This is the inheritance that God left to artists

69.
Before my eyes dripping with quicksilver tears
The mirror shows glass grown puffy from crying

—collected and translated from the Chinese by Denis Mair

from IN PRAISE OF LOVE

and so then
the first moment
do you remember the names
no, no
perhaps nothing was said
the end of a demonstration
and then she's with a friend
who telephones
and then she
to please him

she has sewn a yellow star
on her blouse
and then they hear
there are some guys coming
and then she writes
something
unemployed workers, use the time
to start to think
the guys come
they see the yellow star
they try to tear it off
they say to her
you want to see fascists
ok, now you're going to
and then they knock her out
she's unconscious
and then there are some people who
what a time
and if you were asked
if it was you
if you had a choice

a trinity of stories
the beginning
 the end

kill time
don't budge
mankind is what remains

cinema, theatre, novel
or opera   I'm going
what would you choose
a novel, I believe
good, so we have a project
and it tells
something of the story
of three couples
and this something
is one of the moments
one of the four moments of love
that is
meeting
physical passion
and then separation, and then
reconciliation
and you, what is your part in this going to be
and you
what is your part in this going to be
me, I think

that I will play the young girl
I have an idea
let's suppose she's named
he's named
Perceval
and she, she'll be named
Eglantine
very well
good then, very well
I am Eglantine
very well, good then
do you see the difference
have you understood
that this is not the story of Eglantine
but a moment
of history
the great history
that passes through Eglantine
the moment of youth
yes
you could say

it's a sociological study
for example
when we have the meeting
of the old man and the old woman
it will be in
a soup kitchen
yes, in this project
the fact is, we can't avoid
showing
yes, showing
les miserables
they're everywhere today
the ones Victor Hugo
you know Victor Hugo
yes, of course
have a seat
you can smoke
if you want to
what are you thinking about
I was wondering
if my cigarette would last
until tonight

and also, if my shoelaces
would last until tomorrow
and also
if my breath would last until
next week
you work
yes, a lot
at night too
especially at night, and the night
in the day
do you ever cry
one can understand at a glance
why a child cries
with people walking by
with people walking by
that's how they loved
Albert and Albertine
I don't know, it depends on the idea
that I still have of myself
someone who plans to keep
moving ahead
implicates in his former self

a self that no longer exists
and he loses interest, whereas
some people's plans refuse
time, and a link of solidarity,
very strong, with
the past is created, that's the case
with almost all old people
they don't want
time
because they're afraid of wasting away
each of them, in his inner self

but I don't know
how memory can help us
find our lives again
perhaps the question is not
to know
whether man will keep going
but whether he has the right to

—translated from the French by Bill Kron

THE SPACES BETWEEN: DORIT CYPIS SPEAKS WITH SIMONE FORTI, with an ADDENDA

(From a conversation recorded in October 2003 between the visual artist and mediator Dorit Cypis and the dancer, choreographer, writer and Beyond Baroque author Simone Forti. The first part was published by X-Tra magazine in the summer of 2004.)

Dorit Cypis: As we sit around the kitchen table, you were saying that you are addicted to watching *C-Span*...

Simone Forti: One of my favorite formats to watch on *C-Span* is either the Senate or House of Representative Hearings with people reporting in. They're called "Witnesses." I enjoy hearing Amendments being proposed for legislation, where the Senators or Congresspeople give their thoughts and rationale, then read the wording of the Amendment and then explain exactly what the Amendment would do. Sometimes their thoughts expand around some question that they then boil down into particular wording and particular actions that they recommend. Another interesting thing is the difference between propaganda and when someone is really speaking their mind. I love watching Maxine Waters; she just cuts to the chase and says things that are already on everybody's mind but that are always being treated very politically...she's speaking politically, too.

DC: But using a different strategy. In your book *Oh, Tongue*, published by Beyond Baroque in 2003, you alluded to political events, your family being caught up in the events of the 20th Century. You also describe processes in your dance work of the '80s and '90s, which open up a territory for questioning your sentiments around political events...for example, the News Animations. How did they come to be?

SF: I was at a loss in my work, partly because I had been working with the musician Peter Van Riper, who I was married to. We were travelling together for seven years. He mainly played saxophone, small flutes, and small percussion instruments and I was working with the animal studies and observations in nature as improvisational movement in relation to his playing. When our marriage broke up the work partnership broke up. I found myself with the rug pulled out from under me and I didn't know how I was going to work. Also, my father had recently died, so it was a hard time. My father always read the newspaper; every day he'd read the *LA Times* and *The Wall Street Journal*, at least, and I came to have a sense of security because he would be scanning the world. For instance when the Cuban Missile Crisis happened, I got a call from him saying, "If something terrible starts, we're meeting in Ojai. There's some money in the bank, there's an account for us there and that's where the family's going to sit it out."

DC: Sounds like a man with war experience to me.

SF: We got out of Europe when many people waited too long and weren't able to get out. I think we got out of Italy in December of '38. He was hooked on reading the news. That's how he knew where to invest and when to flee.

DC: The two important things in life.

SF: ....When to get the hell out. So when he died I started reading the newspaper because I figured...

DC: Someone had to...

SF: It was a sense that he didn't read it anymore so I'd better. I wasn't involved with investment and there was no question about needing to flee. My relationship to the information was that I was just learning. I was very naïve and very interested. I started a workshop called *Work In Progress*. This was in New York in 1981 or '82. I tried working with the news in the workshop, speaking out my questions, moving my body and moving newspapers around on the floor to make maps...trying to understand tensions and collapses and things lingering there on the horizon.

DC: What did you find?

SF: Well, for instance, that was the time of the Iran-Iraq War. My understanding was that Iraq wanted the estuary that went into the Gulf because they had such a tiny, tiny bit of land touching the Gulf that they were almost land-locked. That estuary

Dorit Cypis & Simone Forti 49

was also a flyway for birds … and then the human waves, the vision of human waves…I'd find myself flinging myself through space and then rolling with this sense of human waves…the tragedy of it, and also I had the sense of blood soaking into the ground and of the oil underneath—the petroleum which is organic matter— almost calling organic matter to itself. It seemed like petroleum calls blood to it; down into it….and then the Arab Peninsula, I read that it was drifting towards Europe and that's what had made the Alps….so there was a sense of drama between people and larger, ongoing phenomenon around it…

DC: You're covering the fabulous, the spectacular about life and the world, which the newspaper reports on a literally flat surface…always defined by some political framing. You're including that frame but you're juxtaposing it with huge movements that are geographical, geological, psychological, psychic…human.

SF: And also the tension between the Sunni and Shia … that the Shia more the bloodline of the daughter of Mohammed, and that the Sunni are more the line of the apprentice, the intellectual line…that interested me, too. This comparison between the intellectual and the bloodline really changed my posture…whether up in my verbal mind or in my womb…

DC: You're suggesting, in a poetic way, a separation that is mind and body.

SF: And between the powerful and the salt of the earth.

DC: What is held as powerful…

SF: Or what's given a certain kind of power, money power.

DC: Verbal power, language…how that then is embodied by identities. How people embody cultural heritage, history, and tradition in their bodies and live them as identities. This separates them from others who perceive their identities differently or as in opposition, in vicious circles. This has something to do with how we speak; where our intention comes from, where we're speaking from. It comes back to *C-Span* and Maxine Waters.

SF: It comes back to political positions, or where you're speaking from. I was speaking this morning with my mother's helper. My mother is starting to fail and Maria is looking after her in a Care Unit. Maria's there every day. Maria is more right wing and I'm more left wing and we were talking about the grocery workers' strike in LA. She was saying that the unions are nothing but trouble, saying, "Well, but the markets aren't losing money because they're still open." And I said, "Yes, but not many people go in there." And she said, "Yeah, because they don't want trouble." And I said, "Not only that, but they want to support the striking workers." I suddenly realized what we were doing. She was giving me her line, I was giving her mine…

DC: The "position."

SF: She was saying "I'm a right winger," and I was saying "I'm a left winger." We were essentially giving more information about ourselves then about the situation.

DC: The position is only the surface of an identity, the posture. More complex meanings are behind it or underneath it. Tell me about one of the News Animations.

SF: At the very beginning of the first Gulf War in 1991, I did one that I liked a lot. I like to sometimes have what I call an arbitrary object if I don't have the newspapers. In this case I'd found this little, little piece of a board. Just a little broken piece of plank that was book size. Somehow I identified myself with it as being one of the hostages who was holding back the beginning of the war and thought if they could rotate these hostages so no one would have to do that for very long, then I'd be ready to go volunteer and be a hostage for a month. Then once we, the U.S., started bombing, I stopped doing the News Animations.

DC: Do you know why?

SF: I think because I'd been treating events which were full of human suffering with an Italian black humor, which I could do as long as it wasn't my own people that were so obviously causing the suffering.

DC: When you say your "own people," you mean Americans?

SF: Yes....I'm trying to remember how much domestic resistance there was. There wasn't marching and demonstrating at that time. I remember being worried for the American soldiers because many of us did believe that they were likely to get gassed. The next thing that comes to my memory are the Iraqi soldiers trying to get back and being bombed and burned.

DC: Ambushed when they were trying to run away.

SF: That whole highway was littered with the dead retreating army. I remember being horrified.

DC: In your lifetime, being on the left, did you get involved in the politics of the Viet Nam era?

SF: No, I didn't. It didn't occur to me to get involved. I had sentiments but I didn't march; I didn't participate. I don't know why.

DC: Were your peers involved?

SF: I think that my peers early on, that is the Judson people like Tricia Brown, Steve Paxton—I think they were much more involved. During a lot of that period I was more with the *Happenings* people like Bob Whitman, Claes Oldenburg, Lucas Samaras—I don't think they were involved.

DC: Can you imagine what the difference was in political sentiment? What compels an artist to allow their aesthetic practice to overlap and connect with social and world political events, and what estranges some artists from that and keeps them outside as if the are really outside of it?

SF: When I was outside of it, I just was outside of it. I wasn't thinking about it. I'm sure I felt the Viet Nam war was a terrible thing for all sides, but it wasn't in my daily thoughts. I didn't feel that I had any leverage, although in hindsight the demonstrations had a lot of leverage.

DC: I remember being swept up emotionally watching the Czech Revolution soon after 1989...identifying with the artists and the writers who were at the forefront of that movement, including the writer Vaclav Havel who became President. Much of the process of that resistance came from artists working at the foreground. At what point does it sweep us in, and at what point—because our practice does have a kind of built in mental privilege, a sense of "we're outside of that stuff anyway, we're only affecting a certain minor population with our work"—are we distanced?

SF: I've seen photographs of the Judson Flag Show that took place at the Judson Church that Al Carmines was the Minister of. There was a whole evening around the Flag, there are photographs of Yvonne Rainer and Steve Paxton and David Gordon naked with flags draped around them, but I don't know how involved any of them actually were. Having been brought up to feel that I should never get involved in any kind of resistance, I didn't.

DC: Being brought up in Europe as a Jew, it certainly was dangerous to get involved; you were supposed to just disappear.

SF: Yeah. I don't feel that anymore.

DC: In *Oh, Tongue*, there is your passion and questioning of your family's position and the events that they went through, trying to grapple with and come to a clear recognition of what that was. That fed other texts that were about war and more contemporary events—certainly we were way into the Middle East at that time—Bosnia, etc. This focus on world events is dominant in *Oh, Tongue*, and is different from your 1974 book *Handbook In Motion*.

SF: I wasn't aware of it when I wrote *Handbook In Motion*, but later I noticed, I'm talking about the Viet Nam years and I do not mention Viet Nam in that whole book. I don't mention not being involved either. I just was completely oblivious to it. I was aware of it in a certain way, in fact while I was in Canada from '72 to '74, I knew that Canada gave amnesty to the draft dodgers coming from the U.S.

DC: And to war deserters...I met up with many of them at that time.

SF: I took my Landed Immigrant papers at that point too, thinking I would stay in Canada. I was aware enough to take my advantage, but I wasn't going to stick my neck out in any way.

DC: I was also aware that in my studies while at the Nova Scotia College of Art and Design, between 1971 and 1975, the war never came up. The artists that came to teach, whether they were from Europe, the States, or Canada never directly dealt with the politics of the moment.

SF: And finally the Judson work also didn't deal with it. I bet Yvonne was involved in demonstrations, but I don't know that anyone else was.

DC: So talk more about your own recognition, in writing *Oh, Tongue,* of a different kind of sentiment—looking back to bring time forward.

SF: For one thing, I took part in a performance, which was Terrence Luke Johnson's idea, called *War and Variations.* Some of the writings in the book were done in preparation for that work.

DC: Post-September-11th?

SF: September 11th had a lot to do with it.

DC: It was the first Tuesday that you and I were co-teaching a workshop at Cal-Arts.

SF: I remember a student having us walk a circle in a swamp with little radios all around. I squatted down to try to catch some news and I was watching the ants and I was thinking about my impending trip across the sea to Brussels. Making my decision to go really made me feel, "Whoa, we've got to keep going. If something happens, something happens." I can't not go.

DC: You can't flee.

SF: I can't flee. And I think that this got me past certain fears, generally.

DC: In a way it's expanding on your father.

SF: He never did any kind of activism…well, in his own way he did. He tells about a time just before the war at his factory. There was some event and someone was there from the state, the fascist state and asked for a particular part of the land. Father said, "Oh, what a shame. I just gave it to the church."

DC: What a choice. The fascist state or the church—

SF: Choose whom to give it to and run, yeah.

DC: How would you characterize the work that you're performing today?

SF: I did a News Animation at *The Bates Festival*, a dance festival at Bates College in Maine and also one at Bennington College, the transcript of which is in *Oh, Tongue*. Before I perform, I can't imagine how I can possibly do it or what I'll possibly do, but I decide I have to do it…

DC: Is it like that every time? Because it is always new?

SF: My use of speaking and moving has branched out into different areas depending on where I am. When I was in Vermont and had my garden, I spoke and moved very much about gardening, about digging in the earth, about watching the worms, the spiders, the centipedes—all the life that's in the earth—and the life of the plants and the strategic arrangements between the different insects and crustaceans, the strategic arrangements between the plants, and my role as gardener.

DC: The process is similar to the News Animations where you're trying to make sense of this other terrain—the newspaper, your role as maybe a hostage…trying to create these relationships between species, between physicalities, between eras and time. It's very relational—you're trying to make sense of relations and relationships. And making them as they are, complex and synergetic, rather than hierarchical and quantifiable.

SF: Right. They become hierarchical when you want to put something on your table—and then there are the bad plants and there are the good plants.

Dorit Cypis & Simone Forti 55

DC: And they're there to feed you; that's a hierarchy, but then you have the opportunity to reseed the garden, making a circle again. You're neither political and social *nor* organic and natural. You allow a kind of attention or looking, experimentation, placement, replacement, location, relocation, juggling systems around, whether they're natural or cultural. It doesn't really matter because they cross over all the time.

SF: But then again, it's very new for me to want to have some leverage in the human game. I'm just feeling an urgency right now about what's happening, about the political forces in the world, a sense that there is a place where I can add a little bit of my own weight to it...and that it would feed my poetry, in a broader sense.

DC: That's the sentiment that allows me, an artist, to go and study mediation, allowing for a different kind of cross-pollination with being in the world. *(Cypis, a long time artist, received a Masters of Dispute Resolution from Pepperdine University in Spring 2005).* The possibility offered by mediation is the ability to tease out internalized interests which disputing parties often consciously or unconsciously disguise as set positions. The mediator creates the safety and space for parties to participate in creating options for resolution based on interests, not positions.

SF: I feel that I'm living in a moment with my fellow artists where we're a little bit stumped. I don't look towards art so much for inspiration, although there are individual art works that inspire me very much. I saw a very interesting small performance piece at the Electric Lodge in Venice, California. Tom Moose comes on with two stools. He sits on one and he puts his boom box on the other. He turns on the boom box and here's this very strident shouting voice in German…. Da da da da da da! Da da da!!…..and my skin just kind of responds. Then he turns it off and speaks the same text in German with the same intonation, very strident, very excited…obviously he's memorized it. Then he stops and he says, "Fascism does not live in the German language." And then he rewinds the tape back to the beginning, turns it on, and plays it in little bits and translates. You start to realize that it's a sportscaster at a World Championship soccer game that Germany won, and then he talks about how this event was the first time since World War II that it felt all right in Germany to get excited...that anyone who followed that game remembers where they were the moment that they heard that Germany had won, the way in America you know where you were when you heard that Kennedy had been shot. In that moment I saw myself again in the subway station, the moment I heard that. And then he says, "In soccer, the game goes on for a certain amount of time and that's it. So if you're ahead, you want time to fly. You want the game to be over." And he says, "And the word 'it's over' is…" and he said the word in German. And then he turned the tape on again and you hear the sportscaster yelling, "It's over! It's over!" You hear it as *language*. You hear the meaning of it because you know the word now; it's not just these sounds that you've learned to know are German and that you have an enemy response to. The sportscaster was so excited, "It's over! It's over!" and Tom yelled, "It's over! It's over!" He brought me through a whole passage of change. I really heard the language differently, as not inhabited by fascism. The piece was transforming and structurally very interesting, delivering a lot with very simple means.

DC: We need to look at old ideas in new ways or we're just recreating the same. I see this in mediation all the time…it's one of my satisfactions in doing it. I so identify with the things you're saying. It makes me realize that having been born in Israel and raised there, in a culture of European survivors—quite hysterical and quite blinded by their own hysteria, doing the only thing they knew how to do, survive—without the ability to step back, to step back and look at, assess, process, evaluate, witness their own reactions—this continues today in the State of Israel. It continues everywhere. It continues in Small Claims Court; it's not just about Israel; it's not just about Germany. We each collude in our own blindness. But there is transmission between us if we really look for that and recognize that.

SF: That would challenge our sense of identity.

DC: Absolutely…it allows you to expand rather than stay within fixed notions of who you think you are.

SF: I remember as kids taking pride in things like, "I don't like spinach," and some-one else saying, "I love spinach." It's these little things that make up your identity. You begin to have pride in who you are and what your likes and dislikes are, even as silly as something you like to eat.

DC: You recognize yourself and your difference, but if you don't recognize the other in their difference, it becomes a plus for you and a minus for them. I still see you, working in that word you use, "researching"...what's in front of you, what's underneath, above, behind—trying to make some kind of synchronistic sense, some kind of movement—both literally and figuratively, moving through the layered sequences of our lives. I know that today you're moving through something that's very present in your life—your mother and her aging process and her dying process. *(Milka Forti died in Los Angeles, her home, on Dec 23, 2003, two months after this interview was completed.)*

SF: It is coming into my writing.

DC: Writing, you obviously see as movement...something moving through you; you're tracking something. The world of language is the world of others.

SF: Maybe. It's hard to know. When I'm in the car and turn on the radio, I need to hear talking as if the vibration of the sound is physical. Some people need music. I need talking.

DC: You're familiar with Butoh, a Japanese form of very emotional internal body movement...it is about physicality and simultaneously about non-physicality and what invisibly passes through the physical—history, the emotion of history—what's held in the body...memory, not language.

SF: No, not language.

DC: Kazuo Ohno, I remember dancing with him in a workshop in Japan in 1988.

SF: I was recently in Japan and saw a lot of Butoh. Like any form, the masters didn't set out to make that form; they pursued an internal need and it took that form. I saw many performances while I was there, including two terrific ones by Min Tanaka.

DC: Kazuo Ohno and Hijikata started Butoh in the '60s. Min Tanaka is second generation Butoh

SF: And he's very much himself. I think he's a moving, strong artist. I saw perform-ances by others and started feeling, "If I have to see another Ophelia stumbling around one more time, completely out of context—just kind of being sad and crazy..." But the solo that Min did, he did because one of the young dancers who was supposed to perform that afternoon died on a construction crew a few weeks earlier, so Min took his place. The location was out in a field that had been plowed at least six inches deep, so as you stepped, your foot sank down. It was kind of muddy and very fluffy. He drove a pick up truck out into the field and got it stuck and got it going again, got it stuck, got it going again. Then he came out in a black suit and went to the end of the field and stood with his arms out in a signal position. Then he ran towards us across the field as fast as he could, and threw himself to the ground, and slid for quite a ways. Really threw himself. Then he got up and walked back...eventually repeating this about five times—starting back in the field and then going a little further over...running and diving into this earth. And then you notice that he's carrying something … some bread. He walked away eating this bread that had dirt on it, walked away, left the truck stuck in the dirt. And I looked back over to him after a while. He was sitting at the side of the road eating this bread. It was such a connection to the young dancer who had died and who had gone into the earth. Movement wise it was beautiful to see him run and dive into the earth, only like a Japanese can—with no holds barred, no worry about hurting himself—just diving down into the earth. You understood what it was about, you understood what he was doing, and you were very moved by it. In the workshop that I did with young Japanese dance students, we took a walk up the mountain and ended up going up the stream in the rocks and we got sopping wet. We really got "into" the mountain in a very joyful way so that we were working very much with the beauty of taking a breath of clean, pine-smelling air, watching a tiny bug teeny, tiny legs moving across a leaf. They took to it. It was like opening a window.

DC: Butoh evokes death, and you're very interested in evoking life, the incremental, the cellular.

SF: Death is a part of it...but a joyous part of it.

DC: Butoh came out of Hiroshima/Nagasaki. It was about allowing sentiments of death to be released in performance, the grieving. That's why the evocation of death...to allow the pronouncement that death happens. It lives in our bodies, even though we're alive. The memory of it, even though it may not be ours, is with us because we have our heritage from the past.

II

*(This addenda to the interview was added by Simone Forti in
July 2006, after publication of her new book, Unbuttoned Sleeves)*

Back around 1980, before the bombing of the U.S. Marines in Beirut, John Glenn spoke of Lebanon as a "slippery slope." Then the newspapers spoke of Iran sending "human waves" against the invading Iraqis. We supplement our rational figuring with our gut feelings, body English, with landscape and kinetic images that help us understand, communicate, decide. When improvising moving and speaking, a new thought might energize my body, or bring it to stillness. The sensation of my hand pressed to the floor might awaken a thought.

I often prepare for performance by doing continuous writing, maybe twenty minutes, starting with a general area of concern and seeing what thoughts, questions, speculations, images, feelings come up. This gives me some touchstones to turn to during performance. I often audio-record my improvisations and then transcribe the recordings. Sometimes I edit these texts so they can stand on their own.

A few years ago I started feeling that, for my performances to go deeper, I needed to bring my personal sense of literature up to the level of my sense of the medium of movement. I was reading William Carlos William's long poem, *Patterson*, and I started attending workshops at Beyond Baroque. I showed its director, Fred Dewey, one of my writings, an imaginary conversation with my father, long dead. Fred asked for more and I gave him a stack of new poems, old journal entries, transcriptions from improvisations, articles. Out of this he put together *Oh, Tongue*. I edited *Unbuttoned Sleeves* much as I had seen him edit *Oh, Tongue*. It's a collection of texts four of us did while working as an ensemble in two of my performance projects, "Unbuttoned Sleeves," from which the book takes its name, and "101." I placed the writings next to each other, moving freely between texts by each of us, following the rhythms and connections that presented themselves, the research that each of us gathered separately and wrote about. That's what's become special about both these books, that's the dance of making a unified vision out of the parts, creating space between.

For the first performance project, "Unbuttoned Sleeves," each of us found his or her area of interest, the assumption being that any four topics, any four voices, would engage each other in particular ways. Sometimes we would scribe each other, writing down what we could catch of another's verbal improvisation. Maybe a list of words was all we could manage, giving a rather cubist sense of the subject. We each did a writing laying out the parameters of our subject, with an orderly sequence of thoughts, and there were also rambling journal musings. Terrence Luke Johnson chose to mix the idea of the prophet, specifically Habakkuk of the Old Testament, with his own uncertainties and hesitations. I focused on the moment my family escaped from fascist Italy into Switzerland, seeing it, and the world, through the eyes of a four year old. Sarah Swenson chose the topic of war and the experience of a soldier, passionately venting her indignation. In performance, musician Douglas Wadle moved with us while playing trombone and a homemade wind/percussion instrument. His writings touch on the tactile sensation of sound, on identifying with his autistic brother's way of experiencing the world. These were then all edited together. The process for the four of us was very similar to the process I used for myself in *Oh, Tongue*. Coming from dance, particularly improvisation, I'm used to collaboration and to the focus of the work being on dialogue. Plays and novels focus on the interaction between voices, but there the various voices are interlocked as functions of the author's overarching view. What interests me about *Unbuttoned Sleeves*, besides the writing itself, is the space between the voices of our group of artists, each with his or her own frailties.

For the second project, "101," partly inspired by discussion with Fred, I had people chose texts having to do with the general realm of governance, whatever that meant to us, as the basis for our reflections in performance. For several years my interest in politics and world events was as witness to a complexity full of pathos and irony. But since my government's response to the events of 9/11, I've been treating government and world events with an active sense of urgency. I thought of the piece "101" as a kind of Civics 101 course for us. We ranged around many different aspects of the subject. I kept coming back to the idealism expressed in the Declaration of Independence. I read Garry Wills' *Inventing America* and was taken with the romantic notion widely held at the time of the Declaration, that it was human nature to find happiness in seeing others happy. And the notion that good government is that which makes the most people happy. There was passion with an edge of heroic feeling. And love, yes—love of good government—was seen as a motive force. Even as I write this, I feel it in my arms, in the tone of my flesh. Love.

People disagree about what constitutes good government. And there's the question of who you want to see happy, who's included in your body politic. I felt that the last two presidential elections had been stolen...*Grief*...I could say more, but no need. I've been reading the *Federalist Papers*, and I'm still plowing through, getting a sense of the complexity, the push and pull of representative government. And getting a sense of the separation of powers as a protective tensile structure which we are losing. *Unbuttoned Sleeves* deals with that. The posture of pledging one's "sacred honor" in pursuit of good government felt like something we could use today. I've been reading a book, *Where the Lightning Strikes,* by anthropologist Peter Nabokov, about American Indians and their sense of how land and sacredness reside in each other, how that sense shapes ways of life and about the Indians' relationship to U.S. government. And I'm reading an article about a great oil spill that's happening to the coast of Lebanon...

ABANDONED BY ART HISTORY: LOST CONTEMPORARY
MONUMENT RECENTLY DISCOVERED

If we could actually visit Asphalt Rundown, we would grasp an even greater apprecia-
tion of nature, despite the action's potentially deplorable effects. Rather than disprove its
actuality, I'd prefer to consider it real so as to tease out the myriad ramifications of this
and other Smithson projects that challenge our preconceptions of "eco-art's" necessarily
beneficial intentions. To remain art, eco-art must avoid instrumentality.[1]

As one might grasp from the above text—snipped from an October 2004 proposal I submitted for Suzaan Boettger's 2005 College Art Association panel concerning the famed land artist Robert Smithson's work— I have periodically wondered
whether Smithson had truly dumped a truckload of asphalt over the side of a quarry
cliff in Italy, as photographs of the 1969 piece claimed. Yves Klein's 1960 dive out a
window turned out to be a composite image, so isn't it plausible that well-known
"documents" of this event were similarly staged? Perhaps this might also explain the
reluctance of the piece's original curator, Fabio Sargentini, to help us when we were
trying to locate it.

Having included *Asphalt Rundown* in my routine slide show "Beyond the White
Cube (1999)," I've had plenty of time to ruminate about its ecological and conceptual ramifications. While researching *Ecovention: Current Art to Transform Local*
Ecologies (2002), I learned that most eco-artists consider *Asphalt Rundown* immoral,
an act of pathological aggression distinct in art history. This piqued my curiosity,
especially since I was already concerned that eco-artists' tendency to point fingers
not only limits artists' opportunities to spawn unknown outcomes, free from moral
imperatives, but might eventually fracture this vulnerable tribe.

This is not to say artists are free from responsibilities. Rather, artists rarely act
irresponsibly, although their actions may appear unprincipled. I had hoped to
address *Asphalt Rundown* as an example of a potentially "ugly" act that yielded a
"beautiful" outcome, but of course I had no certain proof that it even happened, let
alone any knowledge of its current condition. By framing *Asphalt Rundown* as the
poster-child for aesthetic freedom, I sought to implore people to explore their imagination and test their fantasies, to not get mired in "truth" or "goodness," the respec-
tive domains of science and ethics, rather than aesthetics.

By the time the panel finally assembled, my far-flung proposal had been rejected. Boettger had selected instead philosopher/psychoanalyst Donald Kuspit who interpreted Smithson's art as indicative of undiagnosed schizophrenia having developed into bi-polar disorder. Kuspit cited *Asphalt Rundown* as exemplary of Smithson's "death-drive." Afterwards, I showed him photographs of the actual site, taken only seven weeks earlier in the dead of winter. As I earnestly pointed out the rather faint, triangular patch of grass, Kuspit advised me to purchase the quarry.

Flash back to December 2004. Patrizia Giambi, a great artist/friend who lives in Italy and has worked with asphalt, agreed to help me locate *Asphalt Rundown's* possible remains. Never intending to embark on a "big adventure," I was relieved when she mentioned her friend had arranged for us to meet Sargentini, *Asphalt Rundown's* curator, still in Rome, whom we presumed would take us to the site. He refused, but encouraged us onward, suggesting we could find it, equipped as we were with an outmoded topographical map faxed by Nancy Holt, Smithson's widow, the week before. Fortunately, after travelling outside Rome, the bus dropped us along the quarry's west side. Otherwise, we would never have seen it, since Via Laurentina, the easily accessible road passing along its east side, runs beneath a ridge that obscures all sightlines. No longer out in the middle of nowhere, the site now sits semi-hidden and ignored amidst the suburban villas of Rome's nouveau riche. Imagine their surprise when one Sunday, Patrizia rang their gate bells, requesting the whereabouts of the nearest quarry. Most denied knowing about it.

Following a hunch based on previous photo "documents," we kept walking east, searching for a cliff that resembled our memory of the photographs; accidentally, we had left them behind. Our use of photographs as field-guide echoed Marcel Duchamp's reproduction of "Fountain" in 1951 according to Alfred Stieglitz's 1917 "document" of the 1917 piece. Continuing eastward, I glimpsed a semi-verdant strip that recalled the shape and location of the asphalt flow. We could view the opposite rim, but crossing the quarry was another matter. Entering on its east side required us to traverse a pocked and rocky field, dart through a newly built sports club, then hitch a car ride with a local farmer.

When I re-read my panel proposal—"If we could actually visit *Asphalt Rundown*, we would grasp an even greater appreciation of nature"—I'm surprised at how true this turned out to be. The first question people ask is whether Smithson intended for something to happen. Did he anticipate asphalt providing a sticky substrate for airborne seeds, enabling green stuff to grow? There are myriad patches of green stuff

growing on the cliffs surrounding this quarry, which may or may not have existed thirty-seven years ago. The chalky cliff surface visible in our own documentation is most likely an eroded version of the one Smithson "dumped" asphalt on, though the remaining verdant drip resembles the asphalt's original path. If Smithson had intended *Asphalt Rundown* to last longer than a day, let alone function like a test-strip,[2] he surely would have publicized its location or assigned someone to record its unfolding process. By contrast, Smithson left careful maintenance instructions for the quarry owner who oversees *Spiral Hill/Broken Circle* (1971, Emmen, Holland). Smithson reinforced *Broken Circle's* ying/yang sand form with spikes and planted special bee-repellant bushes to minimize wind erosion, helping to keep the work intact over time. Not so with the monument we were searching for.

The artworld abandoned *Asphalt Rundown* thirty-seven years ago. Strangely, even the legions of artists, art historians, and museum curators who consider themselves scholars of Smithson, conceptual art, or land art never bothered to check up on it. Despite the industry that has sprung up around Smithson, *Asphalt Rundown* remains one of art history's most enigmatic works, perhaps because Smithson's followers failed to envision its entropic course. Had they followed through, art lovers flocking to the Sistine Chapel, for example, only one hour away, could have visited, as they do *Spiral Jetty* (1970) in Utah. It is not merely that no one knew *Asphalt Rundown's* whereabouts. Somehow, few imagined Smithson's dramatic gesture might have caused something interesting to occur. This is, in its way, as peculiar as my having wondered whether it was a hoax. Only eco-artist Patricia Johanson dared to predict that *Asphalt Rundown* might actually have become bucolic.

Wanting to highlight new forms molded by the interaction of industry, people, and landscape, Smithson executed *Asphalt Rundown, Concrete Pour* (1969, Chicago), *Glue Pour* (1970, Vancouver), *Partially Buried Woodshed* (1970, Ohio), and *Spiral Hill/Broken Circle*. Of these five works, only *Asphalt Rundown* shows nature overriding, and altering, human incursions, thus spontaneously immortalizing the irreversibility and unintended consequences of all actions.

1. Spaid, Sue, October 2004, proposal for Suzaan Boettger "Robert Smithson's Dialectics of Death and Creativity Panel," 2005 College Arts Association, Atlanta, Georgia.
2. Other chance planting projects include Yoko Ono's *Painting for the Wind* (1961), Hans Haacke's *Bowery Seeds* (1970), Alan Sonfist's *Seed Catcher* (1973), Kathryn Miller's *Seed Bombing the Landscape* (1992), and Nine Mile Run—Greenway Project *Slaggarden* (1996-1999).

Sue Spaid 67

THE GARY WEBB PROJECT

(For the past year, Jeremiah Day, former Beyond Baroque artist-in-residence, has been collaborating with the Dutch band We vs. Death, juxtaposing his slide shows with their music. The initial impulse for, and first product of, this collaboration was to chronicle the story of American investigative journalist Gary Webb. A reading from the text below was accompanied by music from the band We vs. Death and Day's 35mm slide projections. The images were details from a found newspaper photograph depicting a failed rescue attempt of an antique-hunter in Los Angeles in the summer of 2005. The piece was originally presented at a construction site in Amsterdam, for the exhibition "For Us The Living/Period of Reflection" at Ellen de Bruijne Projects in 2005, and performed again in April 2006 at Cubitt in London.)

*

On June 9th, 2005 three men broke into a construction site in Los Angeles. They were looking for beer cans. Underneath the construction site there had been an old brewery. There were two friends—they collected old beer cans for fun—and one of the friend's father. He went along to get to know his son better. The father was digging and he pulled something up. When he pulled it up it made a space, a hole. Suddenly it made this opening and he fell in, and just as suddenly it closed back around him and he was trapped. He'd made a space, and fallen into it, and it collapsed around him, and he was trapped. And slowly it crushed him to death.

—

On December 10, 2004, in Northern California, another man died. He had been a writer, a journalist. In certain circles he was famous for a series of articles that he'd written almost ten years before, in 1995.

The first paragraph of his series went like this:

"For the better part of a decade, a San Francisco Bay Area drug ring sold tons of cocaine to the Crips and Bloods street gangs of Los Angeles and funneled millions in drug prof-

11-21, Bellamy Straat, Amsterdam. Still #1

its to a Latin American guerrilla army run by the U.S. Central Intelligence Agency."

I'll read it again....

It was a big story. It was huge. Most of the parts of it were not new—there had been articles about the gangs and the drugs, the shootings and addicts (more dead each year from gang violence in LA than in the Palestinian-Israeli conflict)—there had been articles about the CIA, about secret government, about the Contras, about illegal armies. But this writer's story was big because it brought all of these together, because he'd gotten very lucky and found the man most responsible for the crack cocaine phenomenon in Los Angeles, and found out that this man's main suppliers had been connected to the Contras in Nicaragua. And the writer's story wove all these together.

People went crazy for his story. Nuts. There were protests and marches and townhall meetings. A million people looked at the website in one day. The rest of the press, at first, loved the story, then started to go after it. The *Los Angeles Times* set up a team to get the writer, to find a flaw in his evidence, or in his analysis. And so the writer was attacked everywhere, *New York Times, Washington Post,* TV. Eventually his own newspaper, the *San Jose Mercury News,* stopped defending him, and he lost his job. His wife left him. And last year he died.

He was shot in the head. There were two shots. So many people believed that it was not suicide. They believed this because this writer was not the only writer or artist to investigate such questions and then die by suicide. There had also been a painter who made paintings about this who killed himself, right after a big exhibition of the work at PS1 in New York. People began to believe that these suicides might actually be murders. Also, the story that the writer had written was true. He had more or less proven it, the U.S. government itself admitted it, but it had disappeared, gone from fact back to rumor. It was a matter of public record, but still somehow it became a secret. And so the quality of rumor pervaded the man, even in his factual death.

It does seem that he killed himself. He'd written letters to his ex-wife, to his children. He'd taken care of all his affairs in a planned way. And it is not so uncommon for

Detail from slide show.

someone to miss with the first shot. For the gun to be angled so slightly that the bullet bounces off the skull, and a second shot is necessary.

I believe he killed himself. I've seen a video of him from the year before and he already looked half dead, his mustache gone white and shaved unevenly. One eye a bit off, both a little slow, somehow disconnected from his brain. And he'd said in 1998 that when he'd been forced to sign a letter of resignation from his newspaper, he'd carried the letter around with him for a week. Each day the newspaper would call, the union would call, his wife would ask—did you sign it? And he couldn't for a whole week. He just carried his resignation letter around with him. If he signed it he'd never work in newspapers again. He said it was like carrying around his death certificate.

So I believe he did kill himself. And I asked a friend, the only other person I know who would pay attention to something like this, I said how depressing to think he was killed. If you think the government would kill a man like that, that's really depressing. If you take that seriously and let it into your head, and really fully believe that in the world around us the people who try to find the truth and tell the truth about what happens around us are then killed for it...My friend said, and if he killed himself? What does that mean about the world around us? What does that mean about trying to find the truth, or to speak about what happens and why and who is responsible and who is a criminal. And what is a crime. If he kills himself, what does that mean?

And for us the living? To speak of the dead like this could be called an epitaph. The word comes from the Greek—*epitaphios*—and it originally had two parts. The first part is praise for the fallen, to praise the deeds of those who have passed. And the second part is instructions for the living, for what the lesson is, and what we should learn and what to do with what we learn. Goethe said: above all else I hate that which merely informs me without directly instructing my activity. And our activity?

And for us who have or have not been ruined, or sometimes, or perhaps, or maybe, or were once ruined, beaten down, demolished, destroyed, humbled, humiliated, handicapped, crushed, hurt, wounded, sabotaged, broken, buried, bent, burned up, burned out, bummed out, crumpled, kicked, collapsed, cut, careened, creamed, cri-

11-21, Bellamy Straat, Amsterdam. Still #2

sis-ed, catastrophe-d, killed, slapped silly, suicided, surrendered to the seemingly inevitable. Have or have not, or halfway, or maybe, or perhaps, or a little bit. Surrendered to the seemingly inevitable, perhaps a little bit? Not knowing what to do—is that giving up? And instructions for the living who don't know what to do? Who don't know what to do? Who could fall into a hole and be crushed and die?

For us, the living.

EAR

The ear has
   the contours
          of a ruin

a rim opening
   to hurt

the heard
        shock

breaks

a ringmesh
   over the slick

The absence resonates
       with what went down

MAIL ORDER REVOLUTION

the young republican ladies auxiliary won't be performing fellatio tonight as it was-n't in their books they read while in school and it won't be played on piano by a drunken cad whose somebody's dad right here in the mouth of America…while large chunks of dark propaganda are being printed and pedaled by ex nazi opera-tives who dress in their oldest daughters' apparel dancing around with strange paint-ed women wearing fashionable clothes smoking gold tipped cigarettes blowing rings out their noses…rebellious youngsters cling to pharmaceutical products liposuction credit lines only the finest fermented grapes nicest of wardrobes for our downward spiraling minds…it's a horrible dislocated way gold toothed crime lords spit into satanic winds broken legs make for lopsided movements like handicapped frogs put them all together and it's Hieronymous Bosch scenes….go ahead and bring on the double knit wool reptiles and their informationless papers over priced textiles up on the TV's practicing fake smiles…then a man hoists a flag in his underpants for globe weary leaders whose dentures grow tired and assassins blame the grocery clerks on an analyst's couch…rare red meat piranha's teeth "hello from downtown" it's sixty degrees out seed the clouds find someone to finance the revolution charge it order it by mail over a fern bar lunch would be my hunch then pin the cholesterol handles to a dead man's torso cause you're growing tired so blame it all on saccharin jive before time expires…hey ya wanna know something? your outfit's a crime with those Hong Kong blinds bring them back to life in a colorful assortment sprinkled dusted in sweetness and brine it's one mammoth sweeping motion jack splat blowout the end result is this world spins in another direction and then it's some-thing else and piss not feeling well? dipping down roughed up edges depressed? everything is black and blue I'll tell you what I'll do here take these…hey what's that? a troop of acrobatic, well-trained fleas and we've ruined it for all our heroes….

FALL LITANY

marx failed, the big deal fell thru.
my sense of humor failed, no one was there to laugh.
suicide failed, fad just didn't catch on.
simplicity failed, dang.
peace failed, looked just like war.
the war to end all wars failed, 1918.
the mayans failed, civilization collapsed.
the dinosaurs failed, became birds.
the sun went down, came up on a foggy day.
the moon failed, so shut up.
dirt failed, came out in the wash.
your mom failed, look at you, kid.
courage failed, cuz of stupidity.
the president failed, I piss in his mother's milk.
capitalism failed, 100 million africans died.
piss & vinegar failed, the salad remained untouched.
success failed, brittney spears sang.
the very notion of failure failed, into the day.
violet failed, blushed purple.
the moment failed, never ended.
the stars failed, shshshshsh.

when
did
it
start

with
the
undoing of
Reconstruction

From I, PRIMITIVE

III

I put bougainvilleas in my lips to forget my genesis
and I sowed a plot of apples
where there once only lived a woman,
it was Cain with the sweat of a killer
before the vast beauty of the cadaver.
I recited all my prophecies in the language of Babel,
and raised the dead in order to heal my nights.
But no one grasped my intentions
of filling the world with loveliness
and ever since, I have lived trapped in this imbecilic skin
that eats itself with the passing of time.

—translated from the Spanish by Anthony Seidman

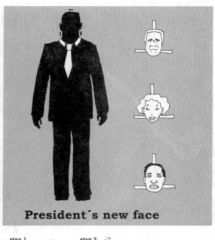

a
little
history

the
special
view
of
history

from REVELATION

In a prose-poetry lecture delivered at Berkeley in 1980, poet and activist Daniel Berrigan presented the historically and critically accurate view of the Book of Revelations—as indictment of the Roman empire at the zenith of its bestial self, as it was encountered by, and slew, people of faith. Berrigan's lecture, "too true to be good," is a timely retort to the Bible's use as a tool to buttress imperial slaughter, torture, and the pursuit of armageddon. My transcription follows...

—Rev. Paul Sawyer

*

the lies
Truth telling "calling the shots"
the shots   simple prophetic words
Demons are persons
not just psychologizing of
experience
dragon   serpent   devil
concealing lies   Satan
the accuser all meet
a yearning for duplicity and
violence in us all
Jesus 1 to 1
early church vs. the society
rejects the mark of the beast (Rev.13)
sign of induction into Imperial Army
psychologizing of the demonic
is demonic
psychologizing undercuts experience
the writing about
the head trip of this luscious
suffering
masochistic alienation
we are skeptical

Daniel Berrigan 83

we analyze
we keep it at
a distance
from soul so "blare"
doesn't reach us
humans possessed by the demonic
every institution vulnerable
to the demonic
every revolution is unfinished business
the court system suppresses justice
in favor of the rich, or racism etc.
cannot isolate Jesus from the
demonic in his lifetime.
a turf being given begrudgingly
unwillingly and bloodily before him
the wilderness   the triple beast
Angels   the oath swearers
the soul of things
the other side of grass trees
and flowers
See ourselves at high level
of spirit
analogies for the spiritual universe
Spirit must be tested
love is the measure (1st Corinthians 13)
The community confirmation and criticism
around having spirit of demonic
possession
the web of the invisible and visible
the angels point to
insane that we can strew the earth
with ugliness and still have the earth

(Discussion ensues on the demonic:)

84 Daniel Berrigan

Is the demonic just anti-human?
Where does it touch on us?
What about holy—God-like—activity?
What are the terms under which we are held hostage?
What is the promise to the community of faith?
How can we declare ourselves free?

TO A SOLDIER'S WIFE

I see you looking at him
In a mortuary in your town
Where the chimneys have darkened the sky
And poverty passes in its black suit.

There, I became a drop of tear
Falling from your beautiful eyes
Onto his sutured mouth
And his torn body
And I became a mournful cry
From your tightened throat
As his casket was carried away
And placed into the shameless ground.

Did you ask his mother
When he took his first step
And what was his first word
And who got his first smile?
His last cry can still be heard
When the American god of war
Put a machine gun in his hands
And sent him to the battlefield:
"Kill! Or be killed!"

I know that he loved you
And tenderness had polished his eyes.
When did you kiss him first
And for the last time
With what dream
Did you send him off?

SCARF

Or maybe an invisible scarf had woven itself, without our noticing, tying us to one another.
—Jean Genet, *Prisoner of Love*

Only in a world in which…....the citizen has been able to recognize the refugee that he or she is—only in such a world is the political survival of humankind today thinkable.
—Giorgio Agamben, *Means Without End.*

On this day like another
we draw the scarf of many colors
from the heap. How it brings out
the colors in your skirt.

For the killed there is no sheltering
and no talk of it. We do not
speak of the dead gathering
where stillness took over.

I reach for, and can't,
the streaked sand, the figure
of the brother at the door with coffee
the flour on his hands still

The memory of the child
in his mother's lap, blood
sopped, those from whom
all that is human departs

(Sabra, Shatilah, 1982)

CEMETARY IN THE SAND (A LULLABY FOR THE IRAQI DEAD)

Between the death
And the weeping
The flies alone
Will be well fed

I am told we can kill
In one second
Two hundred of them
Some, the age of my son
Nineteen, twenty, twenty-one
They will crawl on all fours
Crying for home

Two hundred a second
Too many to place gently
Each in the ground
Dumped two, three, four
At a time
Not even a body bag
Between them and the earth

On the sand
Others strewn
Belching
As they decay
Into withered rocks
Hard, charred mummies
In oversized clothes
Lying in patches
Of their own grease

Before the death
There will be a moment's release
The fleas leave
But then the rats come
Sand
Buried in their flesh
In their eyes nothing grows
And all that is left is
Sand upon sand
Like a mother's hand
Settled gently upon them forever

The infinite sadness of the world
Is the death of its young.

All I want is the truth
Just give me some truth

WHAT LITTLE I KNOW ABOUT THE TRUTH

1.
Truth is merciless and relentless.

2.
As a child I spelled it *f-a-t-h-e-r*.

3.
The truth has a context, a region, a nation,
a history, a sociology, corporate and religious governors.

4.
Daily survival demands much-needed respite in couchings,
softenings, and outright lies. Often, the decent thing to do
is tell the lie.

5.
Truth is often confused with honesty, which is what one gets
when the truth is used to manipulate.

6.
I yelled fire in the auditorium. I was asked if I truly knew the appropriate
signs for fires, did I have fire credentials, and what made me think
that I had the right to yell.

7.
Truth is a commodity or preternatural resource which, when distorted,
fuels the media and national economy as a whole.

8.
It is determined by the quirks of semantics and one's ability to grasp.

9.
It will not necessarily set anyone free. Too often the truth
is a prison, in which the truth-teller dies anonymously.

10.
Hollywood will not finance truths about racism because
they are not entertaining.

11.
As a youngster I spelled it *p-o-e-t-r-y*.

12.
Transforming fantasies and white lies into truths
may become a ruinous fulltime occupation.

13.
My son was murdered by the nation of our birth, the nation we loved.

14.
Truth has a physiology. It enters thru the senses, brains wired in
uncountable variations. What you cannot touch you cannot see.

15.
Presenting it in public forums has not set me free.

16.
Acts of heroism may rule it out.

17.
In my maturity its spelling no longer matters. There are
many thousand spellings.

18.
It cannot be dreamed into existence.

19.
My capacity to forgive has been beaten out of me.

20.
The great-winged condor
      with stupendous beak and ferocious talons
           is settled on my belly, rips out my flesh my soul.

THE TRUTH IS THE FIRST CASUALTY OF THE JUSTICE SYSTEM

The "truth" is the first casualty of the judicial system in America. What do we mean? The truth is the Blindfold we see in sculptures and paintings, artistic renderings of that majestic lady, who, in holding the scales, represents "Justice" for us.

The truth is our axis of reality—the reality of things the way they are and not as we wish them to be. However, there is an inherent problem. This particular truth is conditional on, and by-and-large obscured by, bigotry and other fallacies which produce falsehood. We find ourselves confronted with these invisible enemies—race and fallacy—that we seem all but powerless to identify, scrutinize, resist, or change. Hence, the reality of aforementioned truth—the one that gets us out of bed in the morning and puts us on our way to work—if we are lucky enough to have a job—would also seem to be diametrically opposed to virtue. What do we mean? Virtue is the particular moral excellence of a thing—the conformity to which we ascribe and aspire as a standard of what is right. In modern life, as it is reflected in post-modern literature, virtue has been vandalized by the fallacy, the Pathetic Fallacy, first written about by John Ruskin in 1856, as attributing human emotions and qualities to things.

We have all but run amok in the pure blood sport of politics. We are walking parodies and Orwellian anachronisms from *1984* and *Animal Farm*. Our axis of reality encompasses a precarious point in time. We consider ourselves advanced, yet three-quarters of the world's population have never made or received a telephone call. It becomes imperative we understand fallacy, the process by which false argument is "proven" true, here and abroad, *today*. For example, we are told the reason gasoline is so costly per gallon is because oil companies have not built enough refineries. This is a particular kind of fallacy. We should at the very least be aware of the spectrum of fallacies by which we are run. This includes:

1) hasty generalization; 2) non-sequitur; 3) false analogy; 4) either-or; 5) false cause; 6) circular reasoning; 7) band-wagon appeal; 8) ad hominem; 9) red herring 10) biased language.

There are more.

One of the most important fallacies affecting our freedom is the red herring: an argument which focuses on an irrelevant issue to distract attention from a most relevant issue. What do I mean? The fear generated Post-9/11, the War on Terrorism, and the War in Iraq drawing attention from the invasion of the U.S. Constitution, allowing government, to an extent we barely even know, to examine e-mails, tap phones, and search the homes of all citizens without a warrant. This action is totalitarian because the justice system participates. The problem is not merely fallacy, but rather that this was accomplished by the justice system, even with its minority opinions. This is not democracy but demonstrable Plutocracy, or worse. We mean the fear generated Post-9/11, the War on Terrorism, and the War in Iraq drawing attention from the fact the sitting President of the U.S. is in office based on a vote count never done, rendering his tenure, and all his decisions and appointments, suspect. The decision to not count the votes was made at the heart of the judicial system. Our right to democratically elect a leader is one of the cornerstones of what it means to be an Americans, is it not? The justice system does not believe so.

Red herring fallacy is used around the immigration issue to draw attention away from *preservation* of bigotry, the lynchpin that holds all forms of equality at bay.

Who tells us that a ruling-class does not exist?

Ultimately we must deal with the question: What good is the truth if nobody believes it? If people don't get it because they don't *want* to get it? We are asked to examine this with the counterpoint and moral imperative of why we ought not lie. How do we demonstrate why it is we ought not to lie? We ought not to lie because, when we do, people die. There is another question: how many? We count the mock crosses our consciences have planted for soldiers in the shifting sands that rest atop our ground. We are asked by saber-rattlers who have themselves never raised a sword, "Oh, so you count?"

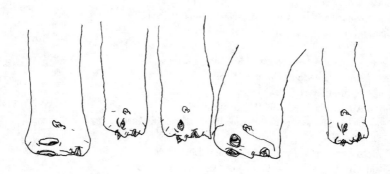

falling stars

THE GOOD AMERICANS

Good Americans are kind to dogs and children.
Good Americans give to the thoroughly needy.
Good Americans are massively patriotic.
Fine Americans express such tender sympathies.

Good Americans have never harmed a living creature.
Good Americans lead basically blameless lives.
Good Americans are proud of their personal karmas.
Upstanding Americans never hear the screams.

Good Americans tend to their own little gardens.
Good Americans don't count their pit bulls
        before they've hatched.
Good Americans breed BMWs for pleasure.
Responsible Americans never drive home through Watts.

Good Americans know nothing is sacred but style.
Good Americans shop at Costco or Wal-Mart or Saks.
Good Americans acquire PCs and CDs and SUVs.
But Loyal Americans own no lampshades of human flesh.

Good Americans are aggressively apathetic.
Good Americans can't hear the children scream.
Good Americans make a business of keeping
        their hands clean.
God-fearing Americans are only doing their jobs.

Good Americans are not their brother's keepers.
Good Americans wear blindfolds on their blindfolds.
Good Americans have front row seats in heaven.
Decent Americans can't hear the tortured screams.

Good Americans ask only that God grant them
    the serenity to accept the things
        they cannot change

    and the ability to ignore
        the things they can.

Good Americans.

WE ARE NOT NAZIS

(Conversation fragments with A.Y.—an Israeli Jew responds to the Lebanon atrocities, Summer 2006)

Write it, write it down, black on white,
To all the Arabs, and the Arab-lovers,
And the bleeding heart traitors,
Let's make one thing clear, first of all,
Before you open your mouths
With comparisons and self-loathing,
We are not Nazis!
And there is only one Holocaust,
There never was and never will be another.
There is no dispute! Period.

What's that?
What do you want from me?
What is this picture?
You want me to cry?
Holocaust?
Go on,
It's not even a massacre.
One child?!
One child—compared to one and a half million children!?
What's wrong with you, are you twisted?
Or are you trying to make me laugh,

So you can say "what an evil man,"
But I'm not crazy, I have a heart,
I am not laughing, nor crying,
But I am mad!
You, and everyone who is behind this,

Are you writing? Write this:
It is a vicious attempt to tar the People of Israel with a broad brush,
But it won't help you!
We're not Nazis!
We are the victims,
Any child can see that,
Even today,
And write this down again:
There was only one Holocaust,
There never was and never will be another.

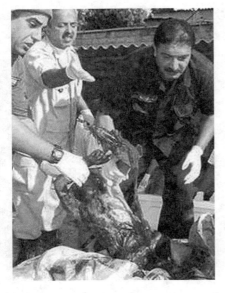

It really breaks your heart,
But I don't lose my head like you do.
More pictures of children? All right,

How many more children? Two more? Three? Four?
Fifty? Take a hundred children, just for the arithmetic,
To shut you up once and for all,
What are a hundred—compared to a million? And I'm rounding it up, for you.
One hundred don't make you a Nazi; neither do one thousand,
And all in self-defense—we're not murderers, I want to make that clear!
Don't turn it upside down
With all kinds of comparisons—
We're not killing anybody,
Were fighting for our lives.
Write, how come you're smiling, write this:
You can't say it,
We're not Nazis,
And there is only one Holocaust,
There never was and never will be another,
Never Again! Never Again!
We won't let you!
Period.

So, what do you want now? Get off my back.

What are you trying to do, shock me?
Where did all those pictures come from, anyhow?
Who's the crazy person who stands around photographing dead children?
Do they have no heart? Beasts.
And where are the parents, huh? Tell me, where are the parents
Of all those dead kids? Before you open up your traps
Show me where in the Holocaust you had Jewish terrorist parents,
Or parents who load up their children's minds
With shit and blind hate?
Show me.

Oh, you're making me laugh. You call that hate?
Aren't you an intellectual?
Innocent girls sleeping for a week in bomb shelters,
And because of who, huh? Not because their parents,
Because of what? Write this: just because they're Jewish.

And show me any hate here? They're just letting off a little steam, so what?
Get off my back you warmonger
And before you open your trap and start all the junk,
Write this for the thousandth time:
There is only one Holocaust,
There never was and never will be another.
I've said my piece.
If you don't like it—
Go drink up the sea in Gaza.
Or in Beirut.
Period.

—translated from the Hebrew: Dena Shunra

Selections from ABRIR FUEGO

If it approaches you
showing its filthy teeth
swallowing a swarm of glass down its gullet
if the city approaches you
with its eye,
(that rabid dog has always been one eye'd),
injecting the same old blood
kick it right in the liver
fire your images pointblank into it
and let it go streak the river with its blood
let it get lost with the shadow shattered between its paws
let it leave you alone
so at least you can check
if on that occasion,
(and only on that occasion),
your name doesn't appear
on today's list of the dead

—

I live on a street with a name
that is entirely foreign to me
I live in a neighborhood with a name
that strikes me as hostile
I live in a city with a name that's
resolutely imposter
resolutely enemy

the names here have declared war against me
letter by letter
                     blow by blow
and I have no other option

but to start the destruction of this city
return to the ancient word
that I hear resounding
like the dazzle of a distant battle
letter by letter
          blow by blow

          —translated from the Spanish by Anthony Seidman

THE LOVE SONG OF MOHAMMED ATTA

America, with four rude thrusts
I have made quick work
of your cherry
seventy pristine vessels beckon me
from the embers of mahogany-paneled
conference rooms on the 103rd floor
for this morning I have unmade you
this morning I return you
to the province of asps and vipers

belly down, America
you are screams
you are mist
you are particles of innocence
you are guilty as sin
mingle now with the asbestos
and smithereens of sheetrock
the subatomic remnants
of a splashy Calder mobile

leap, America,
leap into the glass
and rebar-striated abyss
my deliverance
has blistered your back.
run to the arms of the sky
quick, now!
she is your mother
seek the cooling oblivion
of her fair September embrace

pinwheel like a swastika
feel your morning coffee
still warm in your gut
surrender to gravity
see the water
see the buildings
be the fallout
oh your god
oh your god

history has just cracked in half
raining bombs of pulp
conservative office attire
interrupted routines
abrupt appointments
with the sidewalk
time has fractured
and the damage is exponential

this moment shall repeat in
a thousand billion
upturned tarot cards
a thousand billion
quivering TV screens
a thousand billion
equally terrible ideas
launched to requite
this love of mine

THE LANGUAGE OF GLOBALIZATION

What is in fact a command is entered into as if it were a contract, what is a high-interest loan is received as if it were aid, and what is in fact a lending institution is respected as if it were a donor.

—Ananya Roy, in *Wages of Empire*

We cannot go back on globalization; it is here to stay.

—Joseph Stiglitz, *Globalization and Its Discontents*

How are we to understand the resistance shown by policy-makers in the global North to evidence concerning the violence and failure of their policies of globalization, implemented mostly in the global South? In addressing this question, we need to pay particular attention to the self-identified "good guys"—dedicated, liberally educated, uncynical members of the power elite who see themselves as warriors on the frontlines of poverty eradication, anti-discrimination, and environmental protection. Take Joseph Stiglitz, for example. How can Stiglitz, a Nobel prize-winning economic theorist who resigned from the World Bank to protest its neo-liberal fundamentalism, support imposition on billions of people of a volatile and violent paradigm of human interaction, usually abbreviated as "the Market"? How can he sincerely believe that the Market's stultification of economic and cultural diversity is the high road, as he wrote in his 2002 book *Globalization and Its Discontents*, to "equality, stability, and prosperity"?

The subject position, or subjectivity I am highlighting here is strongly motivated by an affect I call "imperial virtue." "Goodness" or "virtue" is one of the most seductive affects made available by the Western episteme, delivered with an obsessiveness first found in Plato and Aristotle and, in the contemporary world, in the political theorizing of World Bank President Paul Wolfowitz's intellectual mentors, Allan Bloom and Leo Strauss. Wolfowitz's comment upon being nominated by George W. Bush for the presidency of the World Bank, was indicative: "Nothing is more gratifying than being able to help people in need." (*Los Angeles Times*, 3/1705) Conceptualized as a kind of unassailable essence, this "virtue" may be more ruthlessly defended than either wealth or domination, though it often works in their service. In a radio interview on *Democracy Today* (1/26/05), the journalist Seymour Hersh summarized the problematic of imperial virtue when he commented that he had no

Marguerite Waller 109

idea how to reach (in the sense of explain something to) George Bush. "He thinks he is virtuous. He thinks the war in Iraq is the price he has to pay to put America where he thinks it ought to be." The association Hersh makes between the affect, virtue, and a profound unreachability or lack of connection is a crucial clue in appreciating the attraction of the subjective position of imperial "virtue," not only at the extremes of neo-liberalism and fundamentalism, but just as powerfully at the center and center-left of the political spectrum.

The Italian anti-fascist theorist Antonio Gramsci argued that the historical oscil-lation between fascism and liberal democracy in the first sixty years of Italy's existence as a nation state was symptomatic—not of their difference from each other but of their interdependence and conceptual congruence. (*Selected Political Writings* pps. 267-71) If we extend Gramsci's argument to the relation between contemporary neo-liberal economic policy and the positions of many of its critics, we can begin to see a similar kind of co-dependence. The neoconservatives at the IMF and the World Bank pursue policies in the name of productivity and progress—two cardinal virtues of Market economics. Stiglitz resigns from the World Bank and trashes the IMF in the name of exactly the same moral goods. The rhetorical and analytical brilliance of a Noam Chomsky or Arundhati Roy, the ever-growing body of excruciatingly rigorous academic studies, journalistic accounts, and film documentaries of the empirical effects of World Bank policies on actual populations all seem to have little impact. Indeed, they appear to feed the affect of imperial virtue. As long as goodness is equat-ed with superiority, expertise, and mastery, the rule of experts is not threatened.

The tireless performance of imperial virtue is enacted on almost every page of Stiglitz's *Globalization and Its Discontents* and the annual *World Bank Reports* of the last five years. His book's concluding chapter, "The Way Ahead," for example, begins by agreeing with World Bank critics that terrible things have happened to millions of people in the name of globalization. But he categorizes the death and destruction wreaked by economic shock therapies and structural adjustment policies not as sys-temic and system-wide failures, but as anomalous "mistakes," quarantining them safely in a past unconnected with his own position in the present. From these mis-takes emerges a "we" (implicitly global Northerners, though that position goes unspecified) existing now, who can and will "learn" if "we" are not impeded by the mounting resistance to globalization.

If globalization continues to be conducted in the way that it has been in the past, if we continue to fail to learn from our mistakes, globalization will not only not succeed in promoting development but will continue to create poverty and instability. Without reform, the backlash (sic) that has already started will mount and discontent with glob-alization will grow. (Stiglitz/248)

Confronting a present moment marked by difference and conflict, Stiglitz quickly converts those he has portrayed as innocent and tragic victims of globaliza-tion into adversaries. First, as a depersonalized "backlash," their position is cast as a conservative one in opposition to his more enlightened, progressive stance. Then, following the logic of this binary opposition, he rewrites *resistance* to corporate dominance and globalization as the *obstacle* to helping those whom globalization has harmed. By the same masterstroke, Southern malcontent have-nots become a threat to the security and the capacity of the "developed" global North to do good:

*This (growth of the backlash) will be a tragedy for all of us, and especially for the bil-lions who might otherwise have benefited. While those in the developing world stand to lose the most economically, there will be broader political ramifications that will affect the developed world, too. (*Stiglitz/248-49)

Ananya Roy has called attention to the "suspension of critical thought" that is required to follow the terminology of financial institutions involved in "poverty management." In reality, Stiglitz reenacts scenarios of violence and exclusion that he started out by deploring. He has no doubt about, and apparently no objection to, the use of force to impose the corporate development paradigm. He takes it for granted, and is apparently sanguine about the prospect that the have-nots will lose (i.e. be killed) if they assert political agency. We will return to this strikingly desensi-tized response to violence and death below.

World Bank reports bristle with such bizarre transpositions, tricks of narra-tivization, and amnesiac historiography, all of which operate to construct the moral innocence and intellectual superiority of the technocrats at the Bank at the expense of those whom they purport to be helping and who are resisting them. In a compar-ison between the "quality" of institutional structures that "support growth and poverty reduction" in the United States and New Zealand and those in "developing countries," the genocide and slavery at the root of North American economic development are paradoxically at once forgotten and symbolically re-enacted:

> *In the United States and New Zealand, colonizers settled in large numbers and trans-planted institutions common to, and understood by, the general populace, mostly new immigrants. Developing countries on every continent also received formal legal systems, transplanted by colonizers. But their indigenous populations had little access to or understanding of these legal systems. . . .Cross-country evidence suggests that the quali-ty of institutions that support growth and poverty reduction through market develop-ment is lower in these countries than in the former group and has therefore not sup-ported economic growth and poverty reduction to the same extent. (The International Bank for Reconstruction and Development/World Bank, 2002; 10)*

By implication, if the colonizers of "developing countries" had more thoroughly wiped out the indigenous populations and imported a racially distinct, deracinated workforce whose nonparticipation in civil society and institution-building could have been guaranteed during several centuries of slavery, these countries would not currently find themselves in such a predicament.

The "veil of nationhood"

In his prescient analysis of what Italians still refer to as the "Southern Question," Gramsci takes with great seriousness the mediating role played by various "intellectual" discourses in the exploitation, by northern Italian industrialists and bankers, of the agrarian Southern region of a nation-state that emerged from a vio-lent process of "unification" in 1861. Gramsci perceived the unification as an imperi-al venture. Southern agricultural workers who resisted what they saw as an invasion by Garibaldi's forces were defined, and brutally repressed, as "brigands." Southerners in general, whether operating as "brigands" or not, were and are constructed in the North-dominated national imaginary as teleologically belated, as "underdeveloped." In the twenties, Gramsci wrote, "It is well known what kind of ideology has been disseminated in innumerable ways by the propagandists of the bourgeoisie among the masses of the North: the South according to the Northern bourgeoisie is the ball and chain that prevents a more rapid progress in the civil development of Italy . . . . if the South according to this position is underdeveloped, it is not the fault of the capitalist system, or any other historical cause, but of the nature that has made Southerners lazy, incapable, criminal and barbaric. This harsh fate has been only slightly tempered by the purely individual explosion of a few great geniuses." In a book published in 1990, the metaphor of the ball and chain singled out by Gramsci was grafted seamlessly onto a narrative of globalization, whose author writes that the question facing the nation in the late-twentieth century is whether "the ball and chain of the South will drag Italy into the Third World."

Informing Gramsci's analyses, in the *Prison Notebooks* and elsewhere, of the interconnections among industrialization, bourgeois democracy, fascism, class, gender, and other facets of the developing Italian nation-state, is a critique of the validity of abstraction itself. Among these abstractions are those upon which modern economic theory depends. "It is not for nothing," he notes dryly, "that economic science was born in the modern era when the extension of the capitalist system made a relatively homogeneous type of economic man widespread; i.e. when it created the real conditions by reasons of which a scientific abstraction became relatively less arbitrary and less generically devoid of substance than had hitherto been possible." His rigorous skepticism of the "result of a rationalistic, deductive, and abstract process—i.e. one typical of pure intellectuals (or pure asses)"—teases out the evasions and effacements that characterize the discourses on globalization. A double colonization is performed by "the science of economics." Henri Lefebvre, the French philosopher and sociologist, extrapolates the kinds of knowledge-production and political action that this geographical and ideological homogenization promotes:

Abstract space (or those for whom it is a tool) makes the relationship between repetition and difference a(n)…antagonistic one....this space relies on the repetitive—on exchange and interchangeability, on reproducibility, on homogeneity. It reduces differences to induced differences: that is, to differences internally acceptable to a set of 'systems' which are planned as such, prefabricated as such—and which as such are completely redundant. To this reductive end no means is spared—not corruption, not terrorism, not constraint, not violence. (Whence the great temptation of counter-violence, of counter-terror, as a way of restoring difference in and through use.) Destruction and self-destruction, once accidental, have been transformed into laws of life. (Lefebvre, *The Production of Space*/396)

Within such a space, concepts of development, competition, standardization, stability, transparency, history, tradition, and knowledge become an ensemble of inter-related, interdependent abstractions that thickly insulate the "bourgeois" subject (the "we" of Stiglitz's discourse) from the histories, knowledges, realities, and discourses of what are seen and felt as its "antagonists."

To paraphrase Gramsci on Benedetto Croce, the subject of abstract space stands at the pinnacle of a tendentious history blind to the multiplicity of pasts; from this precarious position, the subject seeks to direct the further development of its own "Real." The richly heterogeneous economies of street-level Beijing are of no interest to the highly trained World Bank researcher of "China's economy," who never thinks to stroll through the open-air market that sprawls at the foot of his high-rise office building. Though perhaps even a "Third Worlder" himself, he has so successfully assimilated to the culture of the World Bank that the economic diversity under his nose remains out of sight. This invisibility makes the obliteration of such economies and the devastation of the lives that depend upon them seem ethically and political- ly inconsequential, as John Perkins has taken pains to make clear in his *Confessions of an Economic Hit Man*. The authors of a World Bank report written under Chief Economist Stiglitz's guidance enthuse that "at both the supranational and subna- tional levels, new 'rule-based' and 'transparent' institutions of governance, negotia- tion, coordination, and regulation will play a critical role in promoting a *new equi- librium* between and within countries." (*The International Bank for Reconstruction and Development/World Bank*, 2000) The rules, of course, will be those that favor corporate growth, and the transparency that of imposed, hierarchical homogeneity. None have characterized the solipsistic logic of this ethnocidal, imperial "institu- tion-building" more clearly than the World Bank itself does: "Rule-based processes increase the transparency of policies designed to create desired outcomes and of organizations used to implement them."

The concept of "competition" provides a particularly telling example of this abstraction in action. The World Bank report of 2000 urges, in a list of "Lessons" learned from East Asia and Eastern Europe, that "Competition is essential. It encour- ages efficiency and provides incentives for innovation." Stiglitz elaborates:

When Wal-Mart comes into a community, there are often strong protests from local firms, who fear (rightly) that they will be displaced. Local shopkeepers worry they won't be able to compete with Wal-Mart, with its enormous buying power. People living in small towns worry about what will happen to the character of the community if all local stores are destroyed. These same concerns are a thousand times stronger in developing countries. Although such concerns are legitimate, one has to maintain perspective: the reason that Wal-Mart is successful is that it provides goods to consumers at lower prices. The more efficient delivery of goods and services to poor individuals within developing countries is all the more important given how close to subsistence so many live." (68)

What's left out here is significant. Wal-Mart's "buying power" famously depresses the wages in the factories and sweat shops that supply it. In early 2006, the PBS series *Frontline*, for example, quotes an hourly wage of 25 cents per hour in China; this pushes both offshore workers and newly unemployed domestic workers into the very "subsistence" level existence Stiglitz uses to justify corporate style efficiency and Wal-Mart's destruction of local cultures and economies. He can then downplay the homogenizing and deadly impact of "competition"—the inexorable necessity to standardize, to construct things (and people) as the "same," in order to pit them against each other. The extinction of histories, identities, communities, and cultures is trivialized as a loss of neighborhood "character," reduced to the kind of "lifestyle" issue familiar to a self-centered yuppie. Meanwhile, the further growth of what is already the world's largest corporation (and the subject of numerous lawsuits protesting its practices of product-dumping and of gender and race discrimination) is characterized as an unprecedented opportunity, to be applauded by all readers, performing a feat of great virtue: the "efficient delivery of goods and services to poor individuals within developing countries." Note that, while the offshore populations that are disrupted and displaced are reduced in this discourse to "poor individuals," divested of history, community, and cultural affiliations (Were they always poor? What did they do before the arrival of Wal-Mart stores and manufacturing plants?), U.S. citizens are implicitly offered membership in the exclusive club of first world, corporate do-gooders through their acquiescence to the Wal-Martization of retail business in their areas. It is interesting to speculate how long, and to what degree, Americans will find identification with this image of moral aristocracy a compelling substitute for jobs.

Stiglitz and Gramsci agree on the violence inherent in competition. But, while Stiglitz drives inexorably toward a "perspective" that will make this violence righteous, Gramsci follows the implications of a homogenization that generates its own ersatz, internally acceptable differences to legitimate domination. Competition and standardization are particularly relevant with respect to the formation of "intellectuals," those whose mediating role in economic development Gramsci identified as pivotal. Modernity, he argues, has occasioned an "inordinate" growth of nonproductive official intellectuals—officers of the ruling class for the exercise of the subordinate functions of social hegemony and political government . . . including middle managers, teachers, and engineers—and *it has also standardized them* in terms of both individual and psychological peculiarities." (*The Modern prince & Other Writings*/125) This isomorphism of intellectuals has resulted "in the same phenomena which exist in all other standardized masses: *competition*, which provides the need for professional defensive organizations, unemployment...overproduction, emigration etc.

The "intellectual" subject, the "expert," forged in, and tried by, the fires of competition, can hardly afford to fault this process as it plays out in other spheres. What is at stake is not only one's professional position, but very likely one's personal sense of the world and one's place in it. To think too deeply about competition could call into question the very meaning, and way of making meaning, of ones existence. When this mode of meaning-making and subject construction *are* threatened with deconstructive analysis, the ingenuity and ferocity with which they are "defended" can be breathtaking.

Gramsci intrepidly exposes competition as conducive to the production and maintenance not of prosperity, but of *domination*. Dissolving the abstract noun into its constituent political and historical relationships, he calls attention to the instability and loss to the system or community that the kind of competition Stiglitz is discussing both causes and is fueled by. Competition, with its inherent instability and inevitable exclusions, *necessitates* policing, be it the violent enforcement of physical bodies by police and armed forces or the intellectual policing of bodies of knowledge and epistemological systems by hierarchies of "experts."

Competition "provides the *need*" to create losers. It forces "emigration" in the form of physical displacement or death to take care of whatever and whoever must be ejected from a particular locale to maintain the system. The burgeoning numbers of unemployed, migrants, refugees, and immigrants who are constructed in contemporary globalization discourse as transient, incidental, and anomalous, are not accidental or temporary eruptions of difference, but the predictable outcome of an overproduction of the *same*. In concert with other aspects of economic theory, though, the "losers" generated by processes of corporate competition are denied not only human rights, and in many cases citizenship rights, but their very ontology. In two recent examples, state officials, making "good institutional citizenship in the world" their top priority, baldly denied that people in their areas were starving, despite obvious evidence to the contrary. An editorial in the *New York Times* ("Meanwhile People Starve," 8/14/05) reviews the contribution of Niger's president, Mamadou Tandja—known for his economic orthodoxy—to the threat of starvation facing three million people in his country. "In April, with the famine already gathering force, he imposed food tax increases as part of a budget-balancing package...in an interview with the BBC last week, he insisted that his people 'look well-fed' and that reports to the contrary were 'false propaganda'....." In her essay "Resisting the Semantics of Death: Women, Tea, and Starvation," scholar/activist Piya Chatterjee reports on the elected North Bengal Communist government's denial that 800 tea plantation workers starved to death in the wake of plantation closures brought about by corporate competition. (Chatterjee, in *Wages of Empire*, see biblio.)

What for others might be the signifiers and symptoms of an illogical, wasteful, and unsustainable paradigm remain for Stiglitz and other World Bank policy-makers the "complexities" of economic truths from which "every country will benefit" and become capable of "full development." (*The International Bank for Reconstruction and Development/World Bank*/3).

A state of trauma

The compulsive repetition—and intensification—of historic exclusions, patterns of exploitation, and genocide may not be bringing prosperity to a majority of the world's population, but they do function to maintain the conceptual space in which abstractions of economic policy-making cohere. Those promulgating these policies as often as not believe they are "saving the world" rather than systematically killing people, destroying cultures, and degrading the environment, revealing a uniquely impervious subjectivity to the "virtuous" corporate imperialist.

The formation and the maintenance of the modern capitalist state has been, and is, experienced on multiple levels and by various populations as *traumatic*. The example of Southern Italians, now joined by North and sub-Saharan African emigrants, is paradigmatic. Both are affected by violent exclusions that are economic and discursive. Like our "illegal aliens," the Italian term "*extra comunitari*" suggests not just people who come from elsewhere, but beings who, by their "nature," cannot be part of the national social fabric. If we reconsider the divestment and the globalization discourses in light of the foundational traumas of U.S. history—particularly, though not exclusively, slavery, the Native American genocide, and the 1848 annexation of Northern Mexico—I would read the "imperial virtue" of economic globalization policy-makers as both a repetition of, and a reaction to, the traumas involved in the "unification" and "development" of the mercantilist nation state.

Trauma, according to those who have suffered it and those who have analyzed it, entails an overwhelming sensation of the meaninglessness or impotence of one's subjectivity, a violent obliteration or reduction of the self to instrumentality or sheer matter. The context here is a distinctly Western or Global Northern construction of the subject. According to theorists of trauma (again, Western/Northern), the experience of, and response to, trauma do not depend upon where one is positioned in relation to the traumatizing experience. Victim, perpetrator, witness, or descendents of any of the above, may all become traumatized. The cognitive effects that such experiences can inaugurate have been described, by Judith Herman, among others, in terms evocative of the patterns in Stiglitz's book and the World Bank reports:

Attention is narrowed and perceptions are altered. Peripheral detail, context, and time sense fall away, while attention is strongly focused on central detail in the immediate present. When the focus of attention is extremely narrow, people may experience profound perceptual distortions, including insensitivity to pain, depersonalization, derealization, time slowing and amnesia.(Herman, 1996; 6)

Cathy Caruth, in the anthology *Trauma and Self*, emphasizes that what has come to be called "post traumatic stress disorder" (PTSD) often involves the compulsive *repetition* of the traumatic experience. These repetitions, in turn, have cognitive effects similar to those of the traumas they reenact. Sufferers of PTSD can and often do grow worse over time, sometimes becoming highly aggressive toward others, sometimes, like Holocaust survivors Bruno Bettelheim and Primo Levi, committing suicide. [*Ed note:* symptoms also found among war veterans.]

Theoretical accounts of trauma are sketchy, despite forays into this axiomatically unmappable terrain by artists, clinicians, and scholars such as Art Spiegelman, Herman, and Caruth. What all agree upon is that healing traumatic wounds is a long-term, challenging, improvisational, and non-teleological process, an ongoing practice that depends upon establishing or re-establishing connections with others and within oneself. Caruth, in her study of historical trauma, *Unclaimed Experience*, suggests that as the subject approaches an experience in which its own, or another's, authority, agency, and very existence are overwhelmingly denied, it finds itself in a paradoxical situation. An experience that can neither be remembered in the sense of assimilated to a narrative of the self, nor forgotten as if it had no bearing on the self's sense of itself, this "breach in the mind" cannot be "known," in a philosophical sense or "told" within a linear narrative. "Healing" this breach cannot, therefore, take place in the same conceptual space in which the wound has occurred. Indeed, healing necessarily involves "changing the subject," calling into being a new subjectivity that grounds itself somehow or somewhere other than in the space that has been irreparably violated. Both the wound *and* its potential healing, that is, are threatening to the pleonastic, transparent, readable space privileged by Western metaphysics and the Western nation state.

Rather than suffer the pain of trauma head-on and/or engage in an unsure and itself painful and threatening healing process, not a few PTSD sufferers turn to addictions of various kinds. A sensation of transcendence, apparently reversing or undoing the sense of meaninglessness that often results from trauma, effects an apotheosis of the subject, making it feel like an extra-temporal being with special access to super-human powers. Cultural critic Ann Weinstone, in her study of addiction and transcendence, notes that addiction lends a psychological and metaphysical significance well beyond the high.

Urban sociologist and historian Jane Jacobs, in the *Nature of Economies*, has used the analogy of addiction to describe policy trajectories. In a discussion of economic "vicious circles" that are intended to solve problems but don't, she warns that "solutions" that intensify the problem (for example government subsidies for cod fishing when cod begin to disappear; more roads when traffic becomes congested, etc.) can lead only to collapse: "We should become suspicious of activities displaying these characteristics and seek to cut vicious circles instead of indulging them—essentially the same advice given drug abusers, compulsive gamblers, smokers, or other addicts. Economic vicious circles are economic and political addictions." The only way out, she says, echoing those who work with PTSD sufferers, is to "travel into new conceptual territory."

Jacobs's sanguine assumption that addicts in question will be able to just say "no" to what gives them a sense of well-being and super-human powers skips over the difficulty of recognizing, let alone giving up, addictions. The "super hero" economic policy-maker, addicted to imperial virtue, is much more likely to remain bent on contriving ever more effective means to continue the endgames of development,

Marguerite Waller 119

calling for further destruction of indigenous cultures, further environmental degradation, and further "restructuring" of populations into market subjects. There is no way to reason with an addict using the evidence that s/he is destroying his/her own life and the lives of others. As the drug starts to fail because receptors in the cells in the brain are destroyed, it needs to be taken in higher concentrations in order to have the same effect. When economic restructuring (represented with morally positive connotations through terms such as "opening" markets, bringing poor people the "benefits of modernity," "balancing" the budget, and making governments "fiscally responsible") has led to wide-spread immiseration and often to vigorous protest, the response has been to press forward with ever greater vehemence. Whether this mode of imperialism is carried out cynically, in the ways "economic hit man" John Perkins writes about, or with the sincere conviction that sooner or later poverty will be eliminated by the apotheosis of market economics, does not matter at a certain level of analysis. The more thoroughly populations are impoverished by "restructuring," the more they appear to economic policy-makers to need infusions of corporate capital and "expertise."

It is crucial to appreciate the degree to which the policy-makers of institutions such as the World Bank do *not*, and are not capable of, grasping that their policies actually kill people. More fundamentally, they are in no position to understand, as novelist Jessica Hagedorn has one of her characters put it, "what it means to kill—to take away someone's precious life." This is what is meant by dissociation, desensitization, and depersonalization. The wounds do not go away. The imperial subject, addicted to virtue, is him/herself also wounded and, like a wounded animal, grows increasingly vicious toward anyone who tries to come close to it, whether to help or to attack—indistinguishable gestures from its point of view. In the U.S., now, such wounds are being projected onto the bodies of orientalized Middle Easterners, indigenous Bolivians, undocumented workers, reproductive females, and other less sensationalized targets. It is literally the case that the "we" of the World Bank "cannot go back on globalization" since the existence of this subject position depends upon maintaining the splendid, self- and other-destructive isolation that it seeks to universalize. Whether or not globalization is "here to stay" is another question—one whose answer cannot be taken as a foregone conclusion.

Sources

Cabezas, Amalia, Ellen Reese, Marguerite Waller, eds. (2007) *The Wages of Empire: Neoliberal Policies, Armed Repression, and Women's Poverty*. (Paradigm).

Caruth, Cathy (1996a). "Traumatic Departures: Survival and History in Freud" in *Trauma and Self*. Ed. Charles B. Strozier and Michael Flynn. Lanham, Maryland and London: Rowman and Littlefield Publishers, Inc., 33.

_____ (1996b). *Unclaimed Experience: Trauma, Narrative, and History*. Baltimore and London: The Johns Hopkins University Press, 32.

Gramsci, Antonio (1971, 1989). *Selections from the Prison Notebooks*. Ed. and tr. by Quintin Hoare and Geoffrey Nowell Smith. New York: International Publ., 189.

_____ (1978). *Selections from Political Writings (1921-26)*. Edited and translated by Quintin Hoare. New York: International Publishers, 267-271.

_____ (1995a). *The Southern Question*. Translation and Introduction by Pasquale Verdicchio. West Lafayette, Indiana: Bordighera, Inc., 20.

_____ (l995b). "The Nature and History of Economic Science" in *Further Selections from Prison Notebooks*. Edited and translated by Derek Boothman. Minneapolis: University of Minnesota Press, 166, 416.

Hagedorn, Jessica (2003). *Dream Jungle*. New York, etc. Penguin, 243.

Herman, Judith Lewis (1996). "Crime and Memory" in *Trauma and Self*. Ed. Charles B. Strozier and Michael Flynn. Lanham Maryland and London: Rowman & Littlefield Publishers, Inc., 6, 11

The International Bank for Reconstruction and Development/World Bank (2000). *Entering the 21st Century: World Development Report 1999/2000*. Oxford University Press, 10, 3.Jacobs, Jane (2001). *The Nature of Economies*. New York: Vintage, 87.

Lefebvre, Henri (1991). *The Production of Space*. Trans. Donald Nicholson-Smith Smith. Oxford, U.K. and Cambridge MA: Blackwell. 396, 313. 396.

Mitchell, Timothy (2002). *Rule of Experts: Egypt, Techno-Politics, Modernity*. Berkeley, Los Angeles, London: University of California Press.

Perkins, John (2004). *Confessions of an Economic Hit Man*. San Francisco: Berrett-Koehler, Inc., 24-25, 55-56

Roy, Ananya (forthcoming). "In her name: The Politics of Global Poverty Management" in *The Wages of Empire*, ibidem.

AFTER AKHMATOVA, 1919

"Why is our century worse than any other?"

after the worst of centuries
                    a worse
                              already

ash and blood
              on the brow

when the laugh of an American
                    is an atrocity

when freedom flaps on every screen
                    as the skin of a wound
                                        flaps

NOTES TOWARD A POEM OF REVOLUTION

It is better to lose and win
than win and be defeated.
—Gertrude Stein

1.
What did we in all honesty expect?
That fascist architecture flaunting
          @ the sky
converted now to fluid
              toxic
smoke,   ASH
the long finger of
              impermanence
touches us all   & nobody
can hog the marbles & expect
the others to play

2.
While we mourn & rant for years
over our 3000   how many
                  starve
thanks to our greed
              our unappeasable
hunger

3.
WATER is rising
WIND is blowing

gonna strip the last of

gonna strip the last of
                              our
cheap & awkward
cities

only the music
some of the music
remains

4.
voice of my daughter
quivering on the phone
as she watches
the towers burn

from her new apartment
the one w/ the view...

5.
Gulf War '91, my son
                  @ the demonstration
stops by
                  to eat

Well, we took out
a recruiting station
he tells me
while the cops
followed the crowd downtown
a group of us
split off.

                    I nod &
bite my tongue.   Why talk about
what happened the year he was born?

6.
Wanted a northwest passage
& you've got it, Magellan!
Henry Hudson, A-mer-eee-go,
Da Gama,   are you proud
                          all of you
it took us
only 500 years to melt
the Polar ice

7.
And is it suicide when penguins
give up?   Lie down

8.
Children sold in Africa
in India
child labor laws held barely
eighty years, now
eight-year-olds in brothels   dead
eyes
            who invented
this hell?

9.
Black holes in our hearts

ground zero
        our minds   hands
that won't open   let
                go

10.
Tell me again how many janitors
died in the Towers
                        how many
        sandwich makers'
toilet cleaners'
        families will get that
two-million-per-victim
        in aid?

11.
lost Montségur, we did
lost Prague,   the German
peasant uprisings   lost
Andalusia   (twice)
the Paris Commune

lost @ Haymarket
        lost
Paul Robeson   Spain
even lost   Dashiell Hammett

lost San Francisco   fairly
recently

12.
Chuck in his shorts
watering the garden

gunned down in the Mill Valley dawn

13.
we hole up
enclaves who speak
(again)   in whispers

as they did
when I first came
to these cities

14.
don't mourn
don't organize

strike & move on

ON BONHOEFFER

(Ed. note: Like the earlier Revelation, this was transcribed by Paul Sawyer from a prose-poetry lecture delivered at Berkeley in 1980. Its subject, Pastor Dietrich Bonhoeffer, gave up a comfortable exile in America to return in July 1939 to face the Nazi totalitarian power, eventually participating in an extremely dangerous plot to kill Hitler, for which he was imprisoned by the Nazis, and, after their defeat, shot so he would not live.)

Dietrich Bonhoeffer   moral Lutheran Christian
died in Hitler's concentration camp
private expectation a thing of the past
a more Biblical sense of time
not our debased sense drawn from the machine
a dialectic sense of time:
moves between detachment and attachment
between professionalism and the
requirement of the hour
occasions as landmarks
to mark our journey
signs that lead to realities and
on to signs again
cut fear of peers or
to enter into no marriage contract
except as agreement of conscience
a harsh and modest journey
toward Christianity
and the promise
   A new reading of the Gospel
   the '70s a time of a long sleep
"The way is narrow and hard,
every day as our last
living in faith and responsibility
as if there is a great future"
—Bonhoeffer

We don't dump on our children
our delayed conscience.
We can't dump on them the turnaround
the future will be different if we make it so
—not optimism, a non-gospel business
  of the me-generation
As Paul says: hope is most hope
when it is hoping against hope
when evidence is most absent
the Christian draws upon promise
"Fundamentally we already live as dead..."
—Bonhoeffer

Despair revealed by the immunity of
the bomb makers for themselves:
their mountain retreat
what we most fear is what we most
inflict: expanding circles of violence
A contradiction in our culture:
To live forever or to die and thereby
to live
the promise of Jesus: a passage thru death
We have a dread of death
and the will to kill
We must exorcise this fear
sweating thru it together with our
book open
exorcising death and facing legal jeopardy
jail is the terrorism of the anti-Christ
the conquest of such fear only done together
—separated we become amputees
"Personal suffering a more powerful key
to exploring this world than personal good
fortune."   —Bonhoeffer

Daniel Berrigan 129

He presents himself as a normally
thoughtful courageous person
de-mything himself
not a hero but a modest person
responding to great evil
A way open to us all
an invitation to keep de-mythologizing
ourselves.
People of simplicity straightforwardness
not special   not lacking in esteem
steadfast with each other with a
looseness with the outcome.
Conscience is muddiness and impurity
striving to be pure.
The doors are not going to open
Be patient as the saints so we can
proceed with the calm and realism
The prison experience of trying to read
the Gospel and live it in tough experience
ties together being strong and not in the way
"Who is my mother and my brother?
Those who hear the Gospel and keep it" Jesus
Marriage commonly a desperate grab to
celebrate the culture—then it's the
most degraded sacrament
Marriage must pose the moral stance vs. the culture
In Berrigan's family as related to Bonhoeffer's:
conscience constantly vindicated
before the young
no emphasis on making it
They had another vision
the Catholic Worker rather
than the Catholic Church
the promise:

Eternal Life—not in linear time
but life transfigured
embracing all of time in love's dimension
the marriage of Heaven and Earth
the sacrament of marriage
We are trying to learn the linkage
between last week's action and Ash Wednesday
restoration and Easter
"the hope where there is
no hope."

AT THE THRESHOLD

What brings a person out of his own individual experience, into the collective? What brings him back home? The moments below are my record of that journey, tracing a few of the previous years in our nation's history...and in my own.

June 1999. Pershing Square. Los Angeles.

A white police officer, in his early 20s, stands with a nightstick across his chest. He hardens his jaw, as if to intimidate, but his eyes widen with uncertainty. Meanwhile, an African-American man in his 30s wears khakis, a button-down shirt and wire-rimmed glasses. He sits cross-legged on the ground, as the police order him to move. Finally, a sergeant turns away just as I snap her photo. When developed, the image is blurry, but clear enough to remind me of the disgust on her face.

Not long ago, a friend sent me an e-mail about a "simultaneous street party around the world." I didn't know what that meant. I wanted to find out. So I grabbed my old Nikon and headed downtown. Now I am observing a scene that doesn't compute. Students are arrested, as helicopters hover overhead. Bewildered motorists thrust their faces from their cars. The police hold the line—"don't cross that street!"—as protesters push ever-closer. A rifle appears, and riot gear, and motorcycles with sirens blazing.

This "street party" isn't an anti-war demonstration; nor is it a march for civil rights. Six months before Seattle's WTO protests, it is an attack on the very culture itself.

When it's over, Ron pulls me aside with a matter-of-fact shrug. "They broke it up at just the right time," he says, although we've just met. "Things were about to get unruly." Ron introduces me to Tracy, who isn't quite in charge, but isn't far from it. Then again, she notes the irony of anarchists plotting. Gesturing with her cigarette to the cops ten yards away, she says, "They operate on a totally different organizational principle." Tracy brushes ash from her flowing dress, turns to Ron, whose grizzled face bears several scars. I ask about the purpose of the march. Her response: "To wake people up!"

Earlier, I ran into an old colleague, who dismissed the protesters as "a bunch of radicals." And in this post-modern age, how can we take seriously any group claiming authentically to act in earnest? Yet must the '60s be conjured at every turn—must every moment echo another—or can we think and act separately from what went before?

As I ponder these questions, I snap photos of police officers, marchers, bystanders. I feel the strangeness of being corralled by men with guns. For the briefest of moments, in the tamest of ways, I am treated like the residents of many other nations. Then, I walk away, and I ask myself what I have learned to tolerate.

September 2001. Hollywood.

Two weeks since the terrorist attacks. Two weeks of questions. These are mine: What is it exactly that makes me so uneasy right now? Is it the destruction, or the fear of another attack? The uncertainty of what it means to go to war? The bravado shown by many, quick to plunge ahead? Or is it something more personal? The depth of feeling one day, followed by near-ambivalence the next? My judgments of others: their coping, their grief? Or is it the Annie Dillard questions, returning with a vengeance?

Four years ago, Dillard wrote an essay, "The Wreck of Time—Taking Our Century's Measure," in which she probed the significance of a single human life, among the billions both living and dead. At about the same time, Hollywood released a blockbuster film about the greatest ship that never made it to New York. Together, these led me to a series of uncomfortable questions: What gave our nation the right to impose its will around the world? How could we sustain our reckless patterns of consumption? Why didn't we see the arrogance of our culture, its misguided sense of purpose?

By coincidence, I watched *Titanic* again during that first week in September. My decision to see the film was personal, but perhaps there was a reason my unconscious mind chose to place the image before me at that moment. In the aftermath, while a nation mourns its dead, while each of us carries on the daily struggle to regain our internal compass, I wonder: What will become of us, now? Are we simply doing what must be done? I worry that we're on the wrong path, but maybe it's the only path there is. Maybe that's the awful truth: that this is the only way we could

Jason Greenwald 133

respond. The military build-up. The hardening of lines of division. The effort to turn our nation into a fortress.

I want so much to fall in line. To believe my president when he speaks of good versus evil. To trust in those who say this struggle is clear-cut. But I know better. We all know better. The world is a complicated place. There is no "infinite justice." Our myths may sustain us, but that doesn't mean they're true. Amid all the talk of morality and justice, it is impossible to ignore our own deeds. If we're rightly going to hold others accountable for their actions, then mustn't we be responsible for our own? If justice for the terrorists and their supporters is to be defeated, then what is justice for our way of life that is destroying the planet?

June 2004. Lower Manhattan.

I walked the few blocks from City Hall. When I arrived, I saw the same thing that everyone sees: a gaping hole, where the towers used to be. Then I did what everyone does: I looked up, and tried to imagine those towers still standing. Then I paused, and recalled the image of the second plane hitting.

Men and women rush around me, along with early-afternoon traffic on Church Street. It's a warm summer day—shorts and T-shirts for tourists, rolled-up sleeves for stockbrokers and accountants. I need to walk, but I can't leave the site. It's like some centrifugal force, holding me close. I want to see it, interact with it. So I begin to walk the perimeter. An elderly man offers me postcards showing the towers. I wave him off. I navigate behind tourists who are smiling for photos in front of the fence. And I glare when a young man asks me if I want him to pray for anyone on my behalf.

I don't want to make contact with these people—or with anyone. So I slow myself down, ignoring the motion that surrounds me, paying attention only to the fence that keeps me from what is now one huge construction project. I walk, slowly, with my hand dragging against the fence, as if trying to touch the wound that lies in front of me. I turn a corner, see more of the excavated ground below and in front of me—trucks, men, exposed pipe.

Standing now on the south side of the construction site, I come to the entrance of Fire House 10. A flag waves in front of it, as visitors pose for photos with the firemen. I wonder how many from this house were killed; they must have been the first ones in. My thoughts shift back to the hole that lies before me—both in actual fact, and in all of our lives. Many of us have returned to our daily routines. Thus, a disconnect: in the life of our nation, in the life of ourselves. Five years ago, I watched the protest in Pershing Square. I longed to be part of something, but I didn't have the courage, so I hid behind my camera. Now I find myself at what used to be the World Trade Center and wonder if I am still hiding.

At the end of my walk, on the west side of the site, I pass through the glass-filled atrium of 2 World Financial Center. Badly damaged, it has been restored. Around me, outside, renewal continues. Construction workers haul pipes and tools. Employees from nearby buildings smoke, make small talk, suppress laughter. I can see across to where I began my walk. It is not so far away.

Three months from now, I will enter the Jewish New Year with a task from my rabbi. Take these two truths, she will say, and put them in your pocket. One is: "The world was created for my sake." The other: "I am dust and ashes." For a week and a half, I will carry each of these sayings with me. I will finger them when I need something to hold onto. And I will realize: they are one and the same. Because the fact that I am dust and ashes connects me to the world. It lends a sense of urgency to my endeavors. So, too, does the awareness that the world is created for my sake. Not for mine alone, but rather for each of us. Amid the large forces all around me—nations, terrorists, a global economy—it is comforting to think of myself as an individual and part of something larger. Perhaps this quest for definition, and continuing it, is my way of not hiding.....

FRED DEWEY SPEAKS WITH JACK HIRSCHMAN

(This interview with poet, critic, and activist Jack Hirschman was conducted by writer and Beyond Baroque director Fred Dewey in Santa Monica, CA, summer 2005, as a complete edition of the poet's "Arcanes" was going to print in Italy. The Arcanes is published in a dual, English-Italian edition from Multimedia Edizione.)

Editor's note on usage: as "capitalist" is seldom capitalized, "communist" is also not capitalized, except where institutions and parties are involved.

Fred Dewey: I'm interested in how we can get out of the soft and hard prison that has grown up around us. For the poet, a kind of communication is everything. It's been an ideal. But today, communication is heavily controlled, and invaded, by power, by technology, and most of all by propaganda organizing. You're interested in technology, poetry, and their relation to politics, to language, to a certain kind of energetic spirit and community. You've always been active politically in defense of the poor, the weak, the homeless, and so on. In all of this, in poetry and politics, the problem of truth comes up. What would you consider one of the most important philosophical works for you on the problem?

Jack Hirschman: Well...*The Contributions to Philosophy*...by Martin Heidegger. I think it's his masterpiece. I'm speaking as a poet here. It's got an orchestrated form. It's a fugue in six parts, each part of which is also a fugue. So, there's lots of repetitive overlappings. It has an oracular quality that doesn't exist in any of his other works.

FD: What's the theme, or the subject?

JH: What the truth of being is—*not* what is being. It gets all connected up with the word "*ereignis*," which translates as *event*. It was the most important word he used after the war. *The Contributions* was written in secluded notes when he withdrew from his glaring Nazism, though he was a piggish coward, and remained with the party—whether because he wanted to out-Fuhrer the Fuhrer, or because he was influenced by his wife, who was heavily into National Socialism—until the end of the war. He wrote a book, however, which was not published in Germany until 1989, and was not translated until 1999 in this country. It's still not very known. I just read a tremendous and comprehensive, profound understanding of the book in France, but the book has not been translated into French—which is staggering!

FD: 1989...that's an interesting year to release a book on the subject of truth in being.

JH: You're absolutely right. That was the fall of the Soviet Union. But you can't say this book was like weaponry in that fall because it's no more of a weapon in that fall than in any fall. The premise of the book is that once you go on this journey, well...I like Heidegger because he was a philosopher who wasn't a philosopher. He was a philosopher who was a thinker. Thinking is an adventure of human beings. To think as an adventure...

FD: It seems almost as if thinking stopped everywhere in 1989, and we started rolling backwards.

JH: Ah, you feel that way, huh?

FD: Well, I wonder. I don't think we understand even now, even remotely, what that year was about.

JH: I agree.

FD: I do think it marked the beginning of organized mass delusion in the U.S.A.

JH: There was plenty of mass delusion before 1989.

FD: Yes, but it wasn't organized to the extent that it's organized now, here at least.

JH: Organized mass delusion...ha ha ha! Very good! The point of *The Contributions* is that there were no more systems—that there cannot be. There can't be any systems, there can't be any ideologies, and that's why the book was never published in its own time. He wrote it in a series of, I think, 281 paragraphal notations, and his son put them together.

FD: If thinking is an adventure, how does truth play into that?

JH: The book is about that. The basic premise of the book is that the "First Beginning" is over. And the "First Beginning" is the entire period from Plato to Heidegger (including Nietzsche, who is the last stage of it), the period that is known as Metaphysics, or Philosophy, and which includes everything ideological—whether communism, Nazism, or capitalism. That's over. He wrote this in the '30s, and he was pointing a way to a new beginning. And the new beginning centers around this word "ereignis." And the translators marvelously made up words (because Heidegger used strange words, old German words, even old English ones), and translated "ereignis" not as event, but as "*enowning.*" I like it because it has a pun, "no," in it. There's a very important dimension of refusal in Heidegger. A refusal that's not negative, but a positive refusal, to better let be, because letting be was a very important part of his life. And this word "enowning" contained the contradiction of an appropriation which is not an appropriation. What I mean is, "enowning" includes going through something, but not *not* owning it. It's an extraordinarily interesting word.

FD: But what about the concept of truth? What do you pull out it?

JH: Well, the premise vis-à-vis the Heideggerian discussion has to do with presencing and abscencing, between revealing and concealing, at the same time. There's a dialectic play that goes on. Nothing is not also concealing as it's revealing. Nothing is not unpresencing as it's presencing. And that "coming into presence," which is associated with being in time.... in this book, it's felt and gone through, but vis-à-vis "enowning," to arrive at this idea of what the truth of being is.

FD: These are elaborate philosophical words. What would be a daily example?

JH: If I look at a tree that's there, the tree is there. The tree's presence is something that I perceive. Now, the tree's being then—perceiving the truth of that being is to "enown" its presence. That means a process of going through the idea of the tree, and the experience of the tree. That brings up other things in Heidegger involved with the concept of "dasein," the German word for "being." There are fewer examples of daily application in this book. Of course, that's always difficult in Heidegger. In the essays, you get more of it than you do in the two big tomes.

FD: Let's get away from philosophy for a minute. As a poet, when you're trying to describe your experience (or what you would like to experience, or can't experience), you don't necessarily think philosophically about truth.

JH: No. That's correct.

FD: But the poetic ability itself is all about language, trying to speak about the world, or to speak about an imaginary world. It's an attempt to connect to the world, or to expect that connection.

JH: Yes, that's absolutely so. One doesn't think philosophically as one commences to write a poem. But then, I have to say, all of philosophical thinking is a part of the process of approaching a poem. Indeed, the idea of poetic philosophizing, or philosophical poeticizing, is one of the things that Heidegger's writings have brought forth. Especially after WWII. It's essential. For myself, especially my longer works, the "Arcanes." That's one of the reasons I was drawn to *The Contributions*, because of their fugal form.

FD: What is the meaning of the world "arcane"? "Arcane" in common speech means obscure and inaccessible to ordinary experience because of its style.

JH: No. "Arcane" is "Arcanum," which are the esoteric or occult things and books of the past. But I use it like a canto. I use the word "Arcane" after every segment, or so.

FD: Then is an "Arcane" an act of preservation?

JH: Originally, the first twelve "Arcanes" were published in a book that's now completely out of print. When I started them, here in Echo Park in '72, I called them *The Arcanes of the Comte de St. Germain*, after a persona I used in the first twelve. He was a mystical figure who interested me because he appears in every century. The idea of a spontaneous reincarnation was very pleasing to me. But what I started to do from the beginning was to take mystical and alchemical writings that were interesting to me as a poet and transform them into political realities. As I grew as a Marxist, more and more the political dimension would supercede the alchemical dimension. I remember in '78 writing an alchemical life—just around the time I was starting to really get with the Communist Labor Party. It was an "Arcanic" response to the life of [*anti-apartheid activist*] Steve Biko, who had been killed. I used a lot of images from French alchemy, then ended up picking up on the Negritude movement, on the workers' movement in South Africa—which was very important, and really was the cause of apartheid's downfall. Communism played a big part in the overthrow of the white fascist regime. And I was still using a lot of arcane materials. We usually use the word "arcane" as an adjective now. I use it as a noun. And it also plays on words. A book of mine that David Meltzer published is called *AurSea*. "Aur" is a Cabalistic word of very high import, and "sea" is called "sea" because I wrote it when I was living here in Venice, by the ocean. But "sea" has a lot of different resonances because C is a letter. It's the first letter of my daughter's name. And then "RC" is also Rosicrucian, or it could even be Roman Catholic. So, you can play a lot with the meanings. I've written "Arcanes" which I called the "Darcanes." And then I wrote one for the war in Bosnia called the "Warcane." And I may one day end up writing one called the "Narcane" about the whole thing with drugs in our time, within this chaos and this darkness. It's not anything new in America. We know that it's gone on for some time. But now, drugs are used at all kinds of levels. Even technology itself can become like a drug. The basic idea and essence of my "Arcanes" is to provide a reed in a time of runaway chaos and darkness, within and out of the self. To provide the light of structure. Structure is really the whole thing in these "Arcanes," which might then do a few things: to provide a spiritual strength to the one who perceives the meaning of the structure as one reads an "Arcane"; to point—because structure is not something empty...structure is something that resonates with things of the past. What I hope for most is the most recent past. There is a dignity of the human form which came with the Russian Revolution in its early stages, in certain expressed works, in the Soviet Period—a monumentalized dignity. And I want the structure of my "Arcanes" to resonate with that. That's very important in every "Arcane," although I have achieved it fully on only one or two occasions.

FD: It's going to be hard for us to maintain common ground here because you and I differ so on the meaning of the Russian Revolution and the Soviet period. What happens for me with the 20th century and the rise of these enormous mass bureaucracies is the disappearance of truth, and usually after that, people. It happens in this country, it happened in Russia, it happened in Germany in the '20s and '30s, it happens in countries whether they are capitalist, communist, or fascist, or a mix of all three. We're all living, in a sense, amid ruins constructed by organized propaganda government, by ruthless total states. And when you're living in a world where state power is so enormous and unchecked, how can you find the truth? I understand the ideal, the hope, the dream that this period and the Soviet System present for you, but they absolutely don't for me.

JH: You're correct in pointing out our difference. But I don't know if there really is that much of a difference. When I speak of a monumentalized dignity...I'm sure you can understand, in relation to the early stages of the Russian Revolution (even amidst the horror and the hunger), the defense of the notion that the poorest and most vulnerable dimensions of society should have risen, or been risen up, to assume a power. Now, we understand this assumption of power. We understand the old notion of the will to power, and all of that that really turns awry. We understand that. But within that moment—I don't even know if it existed then, but I know that because of my sensibility as an American, sometimes we'll see a film, or read a poem, and there will be a resonance to, if not something specific in that moment, the generic experience of that moment. I'll give an example. There's a great poem by *[Italian writer, filmmaker, and critic]* Pier Paolo Pasolini, which I've translated, called "The Beautiful Flags," or "Beautiful Banners." It's a poem that Pasolini wrote, I believe, in the early '70s....

FD: It was extremely important period for him. That's when he really began his attack on consumer society.

JH: That's right. Pasolini, as one knows, was gay. But at the same time, he was on a certain level almost "guilty." He was a leader of a cell, or block, of communists when he was young. But he was thrown out of the Communist Party because of involvement with another guy. It was something that stayed with him all his life. And even though he was tremendously rebellious, scandalous, and courageous artistically— that stayed with him.

FD: His critique of the communists went hand in hand with his critique of the

Catholics and of course the capitalists. He was rejected by both the communists and the Catholics, an extraordinary thing for him, since he drew from their critique of capitalism and owed a debt poetically and politically. It put him in a very contradictory position to society.

JH: Exactly. In his poem, "the Beautiful Banners," he goes back through the years decade by decade. He speaks of the '60s and himself and what was going on, and the '50s...and then he comes to the '40s. It's the last part of the poem, the end. And here you experience what I call monumentalized dignity. And what is it? It's the moment after the war in the '40s, that great period after the consciousness of the total exfoliation that fascism had brought to Italy. And then you had these big drives of the Communist movement and the poor people in Italy, and Pasolini captures this with these flags waving, which then blur into the red of the cherry trees and nature. In a certain sense, that's what I mean by monumentalized dignity. I'm talking about the fusion of nature with ideology, the feeling of ideological attitude. This is the thing that interested me in writing the "Arcanes," because I do feel that not merely are we living in a chaotic and dark time, but we're living in a time which, as you said very accurately, is a prison of communication. It's a time where depth and shallowness are the same thing—which is in effect saying that one cannot hear the resonance, that one cannot get to the deeper parts of one's own reception, that one is blocked by the prison of communication. That's why I'm saying that when I sit down to write an "Arcane," I bring the philosophical dimension. I don't approach the page as a philosopher, but I don't *not* approach it as someone who thinks. And again, I'm trying to make a distinction between thinking and philosophy.

FD: Philosophy is often the death of thinking because it is based on ideas and systemization. Hannah Arendt made this case consistently throughout her life; she comes out of a relationship with Heidegger, and her active refugee work saving Jews, her comprehensive understanding of totalitarianism, and then, later, praises Heidegger as a thinker, but as a stupid, foolish person politically, that is, concerning the actual world. I think what she claimed with Heidegger was that he was concerned with thinking, and that this was an example of activity that needs to be protected, developed, and deepened. Thinking breaks through the shallows and goes to the depths, reveals the depths in the shallows and the shallows in the depths, and, most important of all, distinguishes each from the other. But it also needs other faculties, it needs to be present in the world.

JH: Yes, you're absolutely correct. There was a little group situation in France, people I knew and was interested in. It was difficult to make contact with them ultimately because they believed one should not make contact. It was based on anonymity. One shouldn't communicate. Well, it's very interesting that in *The Contributions* Heidegger speaks of people who will be like-minded, but will not know one another. They will carry this charge, if you like, which includes everything like "the instance of the passage of the last God." It sounds religious, but it's not God as it's used in religion. He means it in another way. It's a god who is inferior in the sense of height to man, and yet who plays a central part in the history of being. This is the "Second Beginning." And remember, the whole idea of this book is that there was one beginning, and that we have begun the "Second Beginning." And Heidegger wrote this in the '30s. The "Second Beginning" is not Nazism—for those who might have the thought, "Oh, he wrote it in the '30s, he was a Nazi...."

FD: Let me catch you for a second because, to my mind, thinking and being like-minded are antithetical. Thinking puts you at odds with everything, or it can. Thinking is almost always out of order, it's not the same as logic. It's not at all the same as the idea. It is resisted by those who are like-minded.

JH: Yes, you're right. Heidegger doesn't use "like-minded" as antithetical to thinking (we do have the word "minded" in there). He means that there are people who understand that we are now in the other beginning, or at the beginning of the beginning, and that this can be extended for hundreds of years before being fully realized. For example, we know in the last ten years that, just technologically speaking, we are different. But not like you would say in the previous ten years, "Oh, I'm different than I was ten years ago." We have a sense that there is a difference now that is unlike anything we've experienced before, and technology plays a big part in that. And this is some of what Heidegger is talking about—that there is a new quality to our existence that requires thinking...

FD: ...and poetry.

JH: That's right. And most people are hard put to arrive at either. And that's also one of the charges. When I say for example, "Everyone's a poet," and people say, "Uh, I'm not a poet," I don't simply mean everyone's a poet in the old democratic way, or communist way, which is certainly true. But under that, there's this other reason. It's as if everyone needs to be a poet to try to begin to understand this new stage of human existence. These are part of the things that go on at least in the making of my "Arcanes." My "Arcanes" can be about the birth of my grandchild. That one pops a little closer to the surface because it's called "The Birth Arcane." But within that, there will never *not* be elements or references to this idea that we've been taking about. Because I believe Heidegger was correct, and that we are in fact now becoming finally conscious—more and more people are.

FD: Ever the optimist, you are.

JH: Oh, yes. To the core!

FD: Let's go back to Pasolini, who used the "technology" of film in a thinking way, much the way a poet—and he was a poet first and foremost—thinks in language. There's a *principle* of language there—Pasolini writes about it at length in his essays in *Heretical Empiricism*—that is deeply poetic and art-informed, and, if you will, a different relation with tools or technology. It rejects a scientistic, behaviorist, systematized—politically subjugating—principle of language and technology. It is in this attempt to truly think about writing and filming practice that we find his sympathy for, and alliance with, not academic semioticians and institutional structures and systems, but with common people, workers, and so on. It is a connection with them not as a mass, but rather in their distinct lives, their actual lives, their plurality, and most of all, their right to stories and poetry. His whole existence was dedicated to bring matters down to concrete examples of life among the people, their suffering, their struggles, their stories and humor, to incite their imagination, even to give them living enactments of canonical texts of their literature. His dedication was to chronicling and infusing the reality and hopes of the people and their life in the face of organizations that claimed sympathy for the people, that directed their activities at the people, but did nothing for them. His complicated relationship with the Communist Party, with the Catholic Church, and with the Christian Democratic, right-wing governments and institutions in Italy had to do very much with his feeling that the people were being abandoned in being invoked. This ceaseless invocation, from left, right, center, by religion, by establishments of poetry, film, and so on, destroyed language, meaning, imagination; it took something vital and made it hollow, meaningless, and worse. For Pasolini, it was a total tyranny. This gets at a problem we have in the United States. The people are constantly invoked yet in fact rejected, subjugated and subjugating themselves as mere functions of the system. The model Pasolini embodied, that I think you embody if I can put it this way, is unflinching commitment to the truth of the condition of the people, what Olson called—in a letter to his town paper in Gloucester—"public conditions."

JH: That is very central. It comes with me like it would come with anyone like me in this country because of the blinders the capitalists are able to throw on anything related to the people.

FD: Well, I would say the political/cartel system, but you can pick your own words to describe it.

JH: Pasolini is derided (excoriated even!) by people on the left, although there is no poet—and ultimately, he was a poet of the cinema—who is more respected and cherished. Remember in his "Apologies" (1968) where he took the side of the police against the student demonstrators?

FD: Vividly.

JH: He was aware of what he was doing. But he could not, in a way, help it because he had made a leap. He himself had said that he came from a very petit-bourgeois background—not of the working class. But he made the leap into the working class, as I did too on a certain level. My parents were working people, but they had the petit-bourgeois dreams of the American story. And at a certain point in my life, I made that leap (which is essential) to identity with the cause of the poorest and the workers in this country and throughout the world. Now Pasolini, having made that leap in taking the side of the police, did a very traditional thing. The police were the sons and daughters of the working class. And he also had the classic and traditional

Marxist detestation of the petit-bourgeoisie as, so to speak, revolutionary makers. So—his attack! And it was an attack he was aware of.

FD: But he was attacking the students because many of them came from the upper class and were basically snobs. He thought that by attacking the police, they failed to understand the police were people too, had less advantages than they did, and were struggling to survive in a total labor economy. He was saying that until you address this you can't have an imagination—political or artistic—that is real, that is committed to the world and in it.

JH: Exactly. In the long run, with the way it all turned out, one can say he was correct. But it wasn't a good choice that he made. He was aware because he writes a poem, but then writes a prose piece after which comes an apology in quotes, so to speak.

FD: I suspect Pasolini's critique of consumer society that follows after this is an effort to push his thinking begun in his "Apologies." I think he understood that the ways in which people are drawn into their own subjugation have to be addressed, across the society. That both wealthy and the poor are part of a system that subjugates everyone and destroys the principle of liberty and freedom, imagination and truth, if you will, and perhaps only the poet can really get at it.

JH: You're correct. It's very interesting when you speak about religion. He wrote poems in which Christ plays roles...

FD: Christ was poor.

JH: ...and Pasolini said, when asked about this, that he came from a family in which a sort of natural religious feeling was practiced. They didn't go to churches, or institutions. And he said that he got it from his grandmother, who in fact was a Jewess. And that that played a part in his sort of "natural feeling" of religion. He was brought up Catholic by his mother. But he named the religious feeling in his family as if there was an "unnatural" (meaning "institutional") Catholicism that was forced on people. He was quick to say that it was very different in his family....

By the way, this is the 30th anniversary of Pasolini's assassination. I've read stories that came out recently saying now that it was three to five guys who killed him.

FD: Well, there was probably one member of the Catholic Church, one member of the Communist Party, one member of the Christian Democrats, and almost certainly somebody from the film industry and poetry establishment. That's five.

JH: I'm sorry, I don't think it was a member of the Communist Party who killed Pasolini, even though communists would say, "Well, we don't know how much *Salo* did." [*Pasolini's film version of the writings of the Marquis de Sade, set in the fascist fallback enclave of Salo, near the end of WWII.*] *Salo* had come out just a couple of months before.

FD: But the Communists hated him, Jack.

JH: They hated him? No.

FD: Yeah. They hated him! The institutional Communists.

JH: Oh, you mean because of what had happened before. Perhaps there was that. He certainly wasn't the ordinary communist, but he was a Marxist to his dying breath. And there was even word that he was killed for being a communist—that they called him a communist while killing him. That part of the story has only recently come out. As you know, the guy who killed him is out of prison. He only spent six years in prison, and obviously he fronted a pack of guys. Now, it could have been that the guys—like in *Petrolio* [*Pasolini's unfinished final book, suppressed for years*]—came on a sexual encounter. But the implications are that that's not what this was. There was one guy, and then he was backed up by three or five others who did it.

FD: Why do you think it's so hard to find out the truth about these kinds of events?

JH: That's an interesting point. There's another poet who died the same way, Jean Senac, an Algerian—a great poet whose book I made an unpublished translation of. When I was in France, in Grenoble, I talked to friends of mine, and they were very circumspect about the sexual texture. When there is a sexual texture to things, there is more distancing. Even though you can talk to anyone whose conscious in Italy today, and they'll say, "Don't be silly! Pasolini was done in for political reasons," because he was going to blow the Christian Democrats, the Tangentopoli case, and he did!

FD: The problem, at least as I understand it, that I think Pasolini was beginning to see, was and remains a two-party, left-right problem. The Socialist and Communist bosses were and are in on the corruption and lying, tied up in all of it, even though the Milan prosecutor Di Pietro, in Tangentopoli [*Ed. Bribecity*] was going mainly after Christian Democrats. The problem is not just the right, it's all the people in the so-called opposition who get their little piece. That was partly the point of the Autonomia movement in Bologna and elsewhere in the 1970s. The institutional Communist Party was as rigid and, in its way, as opposed to representation and participation as the Christian Democrats, the Church, the capitalists, and the cultural establishments. Look at what happened; the Christians Democrats were removed by Tangentopoli, then, almost immediately, we get the long nightmare of Berlusconi, the left waffling all over, mysteriously unable to stop him! You could say there are many in Italy who recognize that because Pasolini understood how deep this goes, he was far ahead of his time.

JH: Well, of course he was. He called the whole shot on the neo-capitalist fascism vis-à-vis consumerism that we are all living in today. There's a contradiction. The communist realizes that the age of scarcity is over, that it's through abundance that the possibility of people having all that they need in the world can be brought about.

FD: But it's not just the fascists, Jack. You could say that the society of abundance is the realization of a communistic dream. There's a communistic quality to the consumerist dream you're not accounting for. And that, to me, is the prison we are in, theoretically, practically, and so on.

JH: But it's a prison only because the makers of abundance are the capitalists.

FD: Wait a second, I thought you just said the ones who proposed abundance were the communists? Let me put this another way. What if the principle of abundance is not enough?

JH: You mean, only enough is enough.

FD: Not at all. *Abundance* is not enough. With a community, you can be "poor" and free, and you can be "rich" and be a slave, not just a slave master. Abundance is the dream of the impoverished; it becomes their goal, rather than power. This has been shown over and over. Abundance is a prison because people cease to see themselves and each other as thinking, acting, speaking human beings first, and instead see themselves as needing things and goods and better jobs. Attention is neutralized.

JH: Yeah, but you're fixating on a different idea of abundance. I mean abundance in the sense that technology can provide food for everybody in the world.

FD: But technology can take food away. Technology in some Third-World countries is producing mass famine and displacement through mechanisms of control, distribution, production, genetically-modified organisms, computerized shipping, etc. Then there's the technology of the police state. Technology is never an inherent good. Nor is abundance.

JH: I'll put it this way. Technologically speaking, you can build a house for everybody on earth in forty-five minutes, a prefab. And you can do that by technology. That's good. The only thing that's bad about it, as far as I'm concerned, is that the people who control the idea of housing are the capitalists, who do not want that to happen.

FD: But the Communists were just as bad in Russia!

JH: That's not possible. What are you talking about? You're going to get into that argument again. I keep reminding you that when they had a revolution, it was so despised from the beginning that fourteen incursions occurred in the Soviet Union in two years. The fight of the Soviet Union was a fight to defend itself against what they saw coming down the line. I've told you the story, have I not, Freddy?

FD: Yes, you've told me the story many times. But what is always missing in your story is the presence of legitimate criticism, not from the capitalists, but from dignified, serious people like Rosa Luxemburg and others, that the structures of democratic and public life were not built into the appropriate cause of revolution. You and I are just not going to agree on this.

JH: But what is the basis of the structure of democratic life? Where does Rosa Luxemburg get her paradigms from?

FD: She gets them from the principles of the republic.

JH: *The Republic?* Plato's?

FD: [Laughter] No, no, *not* Plato! The *antithesis* of Plato! In the activity of workers and people practicing democratic life at the grass roots, in every structure of society, so real representation and participation can occur, so the people have space and time for actuality, for action, for communication, and so on. That's the republic. And her criticism was that in Russia it was a centralized, anti-democratic, anti-republican party-led revolution, an avant-garde-led revolution, it was never led by the workers or the people. So in effect it was never a true revolution, and actually became its opposite, creating tricks everyone would use. You know, her classic phrase "gravediggers of the revolution" and so on. The revolution can find itself only in workers and people practicing and experiencing democracy, action, representation, power, imagination, and so on—learning what freedom feels like, looks like, how it works, the kind of work it takes. That is the revolution. In such structures and spaces you have, in a quite literal sense, everything you need.

JH: That's true, but it is rather Utopianist.

FD: It's certainly no more Utopian than your vision of abundance, or your view of the Soviet "revolution."

JH: Except if you understand how that revolution occurred at the time. The first World War was going on! The revolution should not have occurred until there was a highly-developed republic.

FD: That is correct. That is the precise basis of Luxemburg's criticism of the

Bolsheviks. By being forced, and being led by a party, the revolution was not happening. It wasn't real.

JH: I think the point is well taken—but then there would not have been a Russian Revolution until it would have been impossible to have one. In another ten or fifteen years not only would it have been impossible, there wouldn't have been any Soviet Union, period.

FD: Who knows? I do know the principle of truth is important, not at all as a final thing, or a total thing, but as something that allows us to do things, and see things, and imagine things, not correctly, but accurately, so we can see our power. Facts are part of this, even if they are lied away. And this is the meaning of the adventure of thinking. If you're going to think, you have to do it somewhere in the world, among other people, with other people, amidst facts, based on what is happening, not just on ideas and hopes and dreams. To have an active thinking mind is to affirm a dignified way of life at the same time as one holds onto a principle of truth; it cannot be life at the expense of truth. Thinking and poetry interweave, they form the essence. And there are dangers in every direction. Poets think inside the language, with it, they root us in what we need to act and speak.

JH: When one sits down to write a poem, one is very much concerned with saying the truth of him or herself. And within that saying of the truth of him or herself, one touches upon the truth of what one is going to develop in the process of this poem. There will be a truth created, or discovered. Thinking and poeticizing are the methods to arrive at that discovery of truth. That's what I'm doing in my "Arcanes."

FD: Thank you for that, for keeping certain things alive so we can think about them, for your poetry, and for your spirit.

JH: Your welcome, Freddy.

THE DAYS OF THE DEAD ARCANE

1.

I hope for nothing in the light of this
intrappolando in which the day
on which he died,

not simply murdered, but—as with all
who mean much more than they were—
like a whole nation, even a worlD—

assassinated, America's voting to re-elect
a war machine to continue clubbing
and then running over entire peoples.

So here he is, one of Italy's grandest
poets, who's lain in this grave
in Casarsa, a small Friuli town, for

29 years. Six small laurel trees over
him and Susanna Colussi, his mother,
lying beside him in touching irony.

And the sound sorrow makes when
falling through itself and touching no
bottom, with its sadness of blood

and its melancholy of mind in a world
out of joint—not in the sense of not
having one between one's fingers.

or sitting in a joint and drinking away
the downright injustice of these days, but

meaning that a bought and paid-for Con-

stitution, with a grin and gun at the nape
of the world, has among other things
assassinated Pier Paolo Pasolini again.

2.

What serial Days of the Dead to come!
Even kid sister Marilyn, whom he
poeticized so beautifully, is in the

wings shuddering on this cenotaph I'm
constructing of Aztec peacock feathers
six feet long, photos of Marx, Lenin

beside a hammer and sickle flag, Mary
and Joseph and Baby Jesus too, and Jesus
the Christ. And throw in Rumi and King

as well, a mountain of hair and a pyramid
of shoes. It's the pits, it's the pits, it's the
literal pits, it's the pits that rule the world.

So many dead eyes, I think there are more
than stars in the sky, and they're here too,
gathered at the tips of my forefinger

and thumb holding this pen, all the stars
that died years and years ago. My absentee
vote's for them. And nader/nor between

two men of war. Adda venì baffone. Ah,

there you are! Let's have a great DeeoDee!
Diodi. O diodi. Adda venì baffone.

Look at that street-kid, 6 years old, a tiny
accordion in his hands, a cardboard box
with nothing in it at his squatting knees,

singing on Farhadija Street to passing
crowds, and all who take notice of him
are a bank-guard who shoos him five

meters away (where he's at it again), and
a cop standing over him, who gets up and
splits like in one of Pier Paolo's movies,

3.

Standing naked to my waist in the hot sun on
a Baronissi balcony above Salerno, I hear
the clop of hooves, then see—beside the cars

doing their ordinary rounds in the piazza below—
13 riders on horseback, the last one a woman,
some wearing cowboy hats, one wrapped in

an American flag, heading up the street like
a posse of disciples of Bush. O Day of the Dead
tomorrow, when it's over, America, over there,

over there, where all is battery, derangement
and carelessness. What Days of the Dead
ahead! Full of bodies on so many hot corners
 of the world, pieces of shahid and his (or her)
victims, and the bluster and twisted tripe

palavering out of the mouths of the media.

The Gunstitution is speaking: War Vote!
Thug Vote for the gang-swarming bashes
in this desert of consumerism. Goon Vote

to keep Kill on the lips and blow away those
blowjob communist bastards. Beat 'em
with 2X4s, run 'em over with their own cars!

Break into the cowering houses, like the rain
of bullets. Between the eyes. Before they even…
Kill 'em before they reach for…and blow us

up! The Zero within the Zero's been completed.
The Left's a confirmed frog-croak, a whelp-whine.
And the Right is a dirty sun with a big black oily eye.

But Pasolini's ashes, from his burning, burning
spirit of Bestemmia under earth, Pasolini's ashes
rise on phoenix wings of flame and cry :

Bushit! Bushit! Hunward, crasstian soldyears,
marching to the fear. In the dead of autumn
with your mugs and biers.

You who bomb and kill the very origin of Humanity,
you who shred truth and work up vulture appetites
for blood in this carrion world, soon will smell

the blossom of Victory. Its fragrance enchanting you,
irresistibly. Adoringly you'll fall to your knees to smell it
and it will oblige you by blowing up in your dead face.

HEY JACKDAW*

Hey Jackdaw, they say the earth is dying.

Fuck! Fuck! Crumbs, a small twig. Where is everyone? Don't believe it. What? All air. This tree. That one everyone at once one one one.

You know north?

North. North. The shadow a crumb.

North. Earth. Everything changing. They say no good.

Fuck! We fly all around. Fuck the little green ones parrots. They dive bomb.

You know war?

You know war?

No. I've seen pictures.

What? What?

Like calling. Calling. Same thing.

Same. Bug. Crumb. I'm alone. There they go. I go.

Stay.

I go.

The world is dying.

Fuck. You're nuts. Hey you guys! Wait!

* from *Unbuttoned Sleeves* (Beyond Baroque 2006)

August 7, 2006

Dear Fred

I am in Mexico City right now, where hundreds of thousands of people fight in a peaceful occupation of the main square, the Zocalo, and Paseo Reforma, the most important avenue, for a complete recount of the votes after allegations that the July 2nd elections were manipulated. The right wing candidate "won" with 244, 000 votes out of 41 million, a margin probably smaller than the margin of error.

I guess we all know the problem from Florida 2000... and its possible outcome. The quote I found in the middle of the old city, "How to build a great country? By saying the truth," would probably go a long way with the current US administration, packed with liars all the way up to the top. The quote is from Elena Poniatowska, a journalist and civil rights activist who got famous for her book about the 1968 massacre at Tlatalolco square in Mexico. My friend Heidrun Holzfeind interviewed her last year for a project about the Mexican civil rights movement of 1968, and that's when I met her.

Hope you can use this for the mag, and that it's not too late.

Con un abrazo
Cristobal

Christoph Draeger
Hotel Habita
Presidente Masaryk   # 201
Col. Polanco C. P. 11560
M=E9xico D.F.

* How to Build A Great County? By saying the truth."

LET'S GET DOWN

The dream band in my vitals
has a heavy metal soul

Get down! For the assassin Jing Ke who unrolled a map with a dagger hidden inside,
   but his sorry sidekick pissed himself and gave their plot away
For the soccer player Maradona's legs in 1986, one of an angel one of a she-devil
For a man with too many wrinkles for his age, always on the move with his wife and lots
   of unpermitted children
For Du Fu's eternal autumn in the city of Chang'an, if you like it let it be my present
   to you
For the solitude of an Eskimo and his solitary plume of breath still warm
For Zhuangzi who could dream himself a butterfly but I can only dream of Zhuangzi
For the man walking a woman's walk: those transvestites and fetishists also want an
   edge to fly from
For eight black runners like black lightning on an Olympic track, they run for all the
   black people
For poplar trees like high school girls and high school girls like poplars

Let's get down! For my internship at a vocational school when I sincerely believed I
   would be an engineer of human souls

Get down! For Red Star Sorghum Liquor that was popular ten years back in private
   Beijing restaurants, it turned to blue flames at the touch of a match
For Beethoven's ears and Sima Qian's balls
For a drummer like me and a sailor's wife, the drumhead of our skin is dripping
   honeyed sunlight
For a Beijing University graduate student in the median strip who finally finished his
   count of passing cars
For ghosts that died on nooses deep in the foliage around the Old Summer Palace
For a young man whose face is just like Che Guevara's

Let's get down! For love that came like a pizza falling out of an April Fool's sky but
   ended like a puff of smoke

For young Hitler once dreaming he would be an artist
For all the world's soccer fans especially the Chinese ones who can't get it up
For a sunflower but not for a person who has character traits of a sunflower
For old ladies on the square dancing disco as clumsy and lovable as little girls

Let's get down! For an astronaut who made that painful boot-mark on the moon, Neil
    Armstrong laid his life on the line to claim the moon for us all
For a fetus in its heroic fence-sitting posture that refused to exit the womb

Let's get down! For your seriousness over a microscope, you study how many of those
    critters live in a drop of semen
For your amazing patience as you hold a prostitute's hand and explain to her about
    Akhmatova
For the crucial use of a tiny arsenic bottle at a pivotal juncture in Chinese history
For the daughter I don't have, that angel withheld from me by God
For the spoken word performance of a rapist who takes the stage and recites "Kwid kwid
    cries the osprey, from the islet in the river…"

Let's get down! While your river of talk keeps gushing, I get down for that handbill pasted
    on the telephone pole behind you—"Guaranteed Cure for Impotence"
For the merry man of the greenwood, under his shaven pate sparks many a thought, with
    scant regard for the sheriff's pardon

Let's get down! For a guerrilla of the Shining Path, gone to his final rest in the jungles of
    Peru with Mao Zedong's little red book in his hand
For the painted shorts on a naked man, unnoticed by a policeman
For a poem of which 10,000 lines were written and 10,000 lines omitted
For the homosexuals who have made outstanding contributions to our national family
    planning policy
For my beloved grandmother who followed Liu Hezhen, at the sound of gunfire she fled
    into the underbrush
For Lu Xun my spiritual guide, as death drew near he spoke harshly and forgave no one
For the days and nights when the Great Wall goes on collapsing resoundingly across the
    majong tables of my countrymen

For reality that has reduced the Great Wall to a pile of blocks

For downsized workers but not for arms factories about to close their doors

For an airplane drawn in chalk on a cell wall, about to take flight

For mysterious footprints going nowhere on a landscape of snow

For the phase when a toddler in open-seated pants should change to trousers, but he won't go along with it

For the pale features of a boy whose jism was added to Empress Wu's medicinal formula

Let's get down! For Van Gogh's masterpiece "Clogs," and for the unholy whiff I caught from those fang-bearing work shoes

For the burrow full of fleeing crickets displaced by a stream of my boyhood urine

For the round buttocks of my Auntie, who was responsible for my first case of puppy love

For my fantasy of a beggar being the one to light the Olympic fire, of course his genitals would have to be covered by olive leaves

For the ancient Chinese builder Gao Jianle, his blood was singing like a drummer while he rammed those earthen walls

For Ruan Ji and Xi Kang who go together with Allen Ginsberg and Charles Bukowski

For Xiang Yu's rage like a force of nature when he set the fire that leveled Ah-Fang Palace

Let's get down! For Sun Yat Sen's hangdog looks when he turned beggar, pleading for gold and silver coins to clink on that wide, bare table

For Hemingway's toe being flexible enough to pull a trigger

Let's get down! For the first girl to wrap herself in a flag, even the state's rigidity looks sexy around those comely curves

For the day I first made masturbation a ritual of life and found out what bodily gratitude could be

Let's get down! For me born with this dogface, you want trouble I'll give you trouble, a dog's mouth never spits out ivory, and here's to our great Chinese language!

For that line from my juvenilia that reads: "Ah Yellow River, the menstrual flow of my mother."

For my countrywoman's breast shaped like an ancestor's burial mound

For the morning sun climbing across my woman's buttocks when I open the curtain

For all the world's sadists and all the world's masochists, if only they could become
     happy couples

For the pus in my urine sample, it's my pus no matter what might happen

For my awe of your vagina converted to lines of poetry in praise of your lips

On a moonlit, blossom-scented night get down for the young woman who was
     suffocated by a long kiss

For the gleam of a nun's shaved head that embarrasses my long head of hair

When everyone is turning bourgeois, for that cocktail you named "spot of red"

For Chinese citizens who have a fine sense of what music goes with whose funeral

For our reality in which Wu Song the tigerslayer would not dare to kill a panda bear

For the kid who follows a giant into the bathroom to see how well-hung he is

For my childhood nanny—a street-walker before Liberation—I used to be ashamed of
     that, but now I'm proud

For the sharp-chinned Lenin at the London Wax Museum, he got a blaze of light from
     the one who lit his smoke

To the Dunhuang I've never been to and all its cave art I will never see

For scenarios of rape I couldn't get out of my head one 16-year-old evening

For the Tibetan girl Yang-jin-ma, her kind of cleanness doesn't get washed off even by
     one bath a year

For the eavesdropping device installed in my house, I still don't know what corner they
     put it in

When the needle pricks deep in my buttock, for the blush of dawn on the head nurse's
     cheek

For us being under such a system, when war breaks out the whole country is awash
     with shifty-acting people

For the unwashed breasts of the hooker who suckled an artist of the common people

For dust of knowledge swirling over a landing strip, especially after the missionary's
     plane has taken off

For a young man wearing a scholar's robe and round spectacles, he looks like a wrongly
     written Chinese character

For the impressive tumor on humanity's shoulders, it grows weeds, it is hollow or full
     of shit, on top of that wearing a ridiculous hat

For the haystack ignited by lust on the great northern plain, I never went through that myself

Let's get down! For the owner of an herbal medicine shop, the phlegm rattles in his chest but he does not forget to suck on a water pipe, so who am I to burst in on him, I've been taking the wrong drugs, the fence

Let's get down! For my teenage years of running to meet every ball that rolled my way, and my coach in the sunset light, and our practice goal drawn on a wall in chalk

For a mother saying "Good child, you've had your fill so don't fuss," and somehow this starts me thinking of our country's people

For the prison I found taking the long way round, when it was practically next door to us

For the dwellers deep in subway tunnels who notice our above-ground beastliness

For Qu Yuan's dive into the Miluo River, it was no longer a question of graceful form

For the grand scheme I once harbored that was going to liberate human monsters

For my girl cousin's eyes, since she was small I could see albino crows fly from them, straight into the sky

For hatred in an orphan's bosom that can turn in any direction

For the truths that get me arguing with any stupid jerk until my ears turn red

For weeping rainfall that flies back against every pair of teary eyes

For the gecko I chased madly around the room, the tail I pulled off regenerated later

For ordinary mothers that day in the hospital, and then I showed up, bringing in my son for his circumcision

For the real-life comedy of a guy bragging at a restaurant, he got reported for murder by the fellow at the next table

For the billboard that got half-painted and became part of our cityscape

For the couple I bumped into inside the air-raid tunnel when I snuck in to steal watermelons

For the treacherous anesthetic that lost effect during my operation, so I found out what it really means to howl

For summer scenery when you pedal madly around the city hauling a pedicab driver

For Li Bai hunkering on the peak of Taibai Moutain, even while moving his bowels he does not stop his chess game with Du Fu

For the novel I did not finish, titled *Do Your Worst, Lounge Singers, I Can Take It*

For the neighbor lady who howls in bed every night, by day she takes serious charge of the Party's local organization department

Let's get down! For a grimy boy beneath an off-color streetlight, stripped to his
    underpants, bent over a pool table, wipes nose on hand, one shot and he drops it
    in the pocket
For you telling me like it is, that I'm already beyond help
For my great discovery that happened when she untied her scarf, a big adam's apple
    was bobbing in her neck
For a baby captivated by a tiger, crying rraauuw and crawling forward at top speed

Let's get down! For Ni-er's fine composition "March of the Volunteers" and for my
    beloved woman bawling out loud when her climax comes

—translated from the Chinese by Denis Mair

From: ALIENS

the condensed truth
Pet Milk infinitude
cow into cow into cow
into can into can into
iconic exaltation

sugar gear shift
lifts downfallen
into sweet sweat
relief belief
spasm's 'I AM'
& forget or remember
iambic pent-up

        ·

re-member torn away
wings & thing
that danced
on illumined stages

        ·

the stuff which unpuffs & blurts out intestines & the usual FX

the stuff which means nothing
but everything
the stuff which decays & is poetry
the goo the snot the rot

alive as we die
no myth but being
no being but myth
no no
die to be
to birth

to burst
forth

     •

'otherness'
alias moniker
masked vapor
unknowable
'belonging to
another person
another place' something else
not knowable
a distraction from what is
a challenge
a threat
the obvious

     •

life heat of all internal organs grinds down to soot
bone cold hexagram telegrams
dot dot common amnesia
aphasia dementia
can't remember
can't forget
what is it
who
me?

cape me
big brim hat me
mask me
ask me the meaning of life
& if I say strife
tire-shoe me
retire me
as long as you know

nothing rules
only unknowing
opens up the books
rescrambles the letters
chains them back to fetters
stutter to blank melody
dots chained to staffs
horizontal lines
ruled

.

each amazed wing feather
spread & fanned &
plucked for pens
whose bone nibs dip
deep into inkwells

.

holy moly chain saw
grinds noisily thru
all crapola & viscera
over & over again
w/out merit or meaning

heroic ones stagger out
to shout invincible
to invisible forces
despair breaks through
unrepairable damage
rage burns the pages of holy
broken & unspoken for
no way to make sense to
wounds refusing to heal
to heel

.

Up against the wall
Caligari style
to slide away
duck spotlights
angry driven dogs
dissolve in dark cover

set apart from
what beholds
& holds all
together
in the vision
of blank
sight of
vapor ineffable
w/ affable spew
of metaphor's faith
in lingo to link
all together in one
pure mirrored wall

.

The opinions of people concerning prophecy are like their opinions
concerning the eternity of the world or its creation in time

yes yes
why wait when
time breaks down
fails to exist
in axes of remove
chop chop
your hand reaching out for
            the promised land

David Meltzer 171

GOOD

Elusive. At odds with the absolute despite arguments to the contrary.

Good has a reputation for being boring even though it never takes
the easy way out.

Don't believe it. Don't believe much of what you hear, including this.

I'll continue; there might be some good in it.

Good has difficulty with shape. You can't see goodness. Only examples of it, the way
a bridge demonstrates geometry.

Good can't see you either.

Abstract; hence hard to pin down. Closer to the unknown than we care to admit.

Many people are certain about what is good. How do they manage it?

Good is associated with the color white. Forget that.

Good is also associated with light. This is okay, since light covers
the whole spectrum.

Scan, like a radio telescope, for little dots in immense galaxies.

Synonyms: expand, swirl.

Good is easily personified. Angels. Your cat, a favorite food, friends, and so forth.

Is it really that subjective?

Actually, good can be anything, since anything can be good.

But then, the same goes for bad.

REASON IS CRUEL

Reason
Is cruel
Nuance, the terrible facts
Are the greatest liars,
Memory, you will recall:
Not true.
The oldest stories
Have been found to have
No history, and
What happens in between
Logic erases.
Even the end of the world,
As the beginning—
A false poem—
Will leave only you, my love.
No night,
No moon,
Only you.

THE HOLY FOOL

I had intended to begin by pointing out that you were frightened and unhappy. I was going to list your sufferings, your hang-ups; the ten thousand things that keep your mind in a perpetual turmoil. But that's not necessary. If there is one thing you know, it is that you are miserable. If there is one thing to which you are devoted, it is to discovering ways to ease your misery. So I would only be talking about what you already know. You know in your hearts that your world has become a huge jail, a diabolical prison complete with all the most scientific instruments of torture. we don't have to dwell on that. Instead, I want to tell you how to escape.

The word "escape" has taken on some very bad connotations in recent years. An escapist is a coward or a misguided person, in short, a fool. The priests and the psychiatrists, members of the Universal Confraternity of Prison Guards, will tell you that escapism is sinful or neurotic. They say, "Be good prisoners. Face up to your life sentence. Don't waste our time sawing on the bars of your cell. Earn, instead, the honorable title of "Model Prisoner." Stop digging tunnels under the walls. Don't be fools!" If you persist, of course, you are punished. And the greatest punishment, as they well know, is solitary confinement on bread and water. Only the most hardened troublemakers can endure that.

Escape—practically a dirty word...But I want to tell you how it is done. It is really very simple. It is just a matter of making yourself invisible, transparent, and then walking through the wall! (You were warned that this talk would deal with foolishness, so don't complain!)

Become invisible, become transparent, then simply walk through the walls. And now, the techniques of invisibility. You have built up, over the years, an attitude towards the world. Let it die. You have learned, over the years, ten thousand things about life. Forget them all. You have devised ways of speaking to people, of dealing with them on a verbal level. Forget all the tricks. You have learned how to act—have studied the proper behavior for a model prisoner. Drop it. You have learned how to earn your beans and jail coffee—have you become a skilled worker in the prison tailor shop? Forget all the skills they taught you. They won't help you to escape. Drop it. Drop it all. Apply yourself only to the end of escaping. You are no longer a part of the system. You are now a potential escapee. Fix your mind and your heart on that. Contemplate nothing but escape.

You will try to argue with me. You will tell me how soiled the walls are, how alert the guards are, how absurd it is to practice invisibility. If you are really dishonest you will maintain that this isn't even a jail. My only answer is to point through the barred windows of the cell. See! They are walking around out there, free! They made it. If it has been done before it can be done again. You are awed by the walls, by the guards, by the threat of solitary confinement. I see only the free ones, the ones who walked through the walls and enjoy the open air all day.

Historically, Zen is a method of release that came from India to China in the sixth century A.D., then to Japan some centuries later. Historically, it is traceable to the teachings of the Buddha and of the Chinese Taoist philosophers. In Japan it took on certain aspects of Jaene thought. But that's not important. It has always been accessible. I was turned on to it in San Antonio, Texas, by a queer bookseller. You may be turned on in this silly establishment by my words—and I am no Buddha, no philosopher, not even a proper fool. I hear that one of the Kyoto Zen masters is studying English right now, and that next year he will come to start a monastery in Los Angeles. But that is probably not important either. The important thing is release, escape, realization, enlightenment, satori—many different ways of expressing one—even the only—important event in the world.

What is he like, this holy fool, this man who has attained enlightenment? What are his qualities? What describes him? What is it like to be invisible?

First, he is free. He floats with the currents like a jellyfish, and yet he is free. Prisons have ceased to clutch at them. He is free, like a gas which expands to fit any container. All of space is his home, and it is food, and he is...not happy, but beyond happiness—he is blissful. He is free. He is immortal. No, this doesn't mean he will go to some sugar-candy heaven when he dies, and spend eternity singing Sunday-school ditties to a bearded father-image. No. He is immortal because birth and death no longer exist for him. Everything is NOW, this present pure and blissful moment, and there is no death in the world of NOW. He knows no fear, no anxiety, no ambition, no hate, no greed or envy. He has passed through the iron wall of such hankerings. There are no frontiers for him. He has no shame, no modesty, no pride. He has no needs.

He appears in the world, of course, as a fool. His life is common and anonymous. When he is hungry, he eats; when he is sleepy, he goes to sleep; when the time for action comes, he acts; when there is no reason for action, he sits quietly, doing nothing. It is all the same to him; it is all one. He is, in this urgent world, a fool.

In his conversation he is foolish. Don't expect subtle philosophies to flow from his lips. He makes no neat verbal distinctions. He has no polite phrases. He offers you no answers. He IS the answer, in the flesh. It does no good to ask him about Buddhism. He is not in that prison and doesn't know anything about it. It does no good to ask him about Zen. Zen doesn't exist for him. He has arrived. He has made it. He is where philosophy, religion, morality, birth, and death mean nothing anymore. He is free. He is a fool. He is a saint.

NIGHT PRAYER FOR VARIOUS TRADES

Machinist in the pillow's grip,
Be clumsy and be blind
And let the gears spin free, and turn
No metal in your mind.

Long, long may the actress lie
In slumber like a stone,
The helpless words that rise from sleep
Be no words but her own.

Laborer, drift through a dark
Remote from clay and lime.
O do not tunnel through the night
In unpaid overtime.

You out-of-work, walk into sleep.
It will not ask to see
Your proof of skill or strength or youth
And shows its movies free.

And may the streetcleaner float down
A spotless avenue.
Who red-eyed wake at morning break
All have enough to do.

Enough to do. Now let the day
Its own accountings keep.
But may our dreams keep other time
Throughout our sprawling sleep.

AN INHERITANCE

"Five dollars, four dollars, three dollars, two,
One, and none, and what do we do?"

This is the worry that never got said
But ran so often in my mother's head

And showed so plain in my father's frown
That to us kids it drifted down.

It drifted down like soot, like snow,
In the dream-tossed Bronx, in the long ago.

I shook it off with a shake of the head.
I bounced my ball, I ate warm bread,

I skated down the steepest hill.
But I must have listened, against my will:

When the wind blows wrong, I can hear it today.
Then my mother's worry stops all play

And, as if in its rightful place,
My father's frown divides my face.

FRIENDLY FIRE

The Statue of Liberty is
grieving. She has seen enough
purple majesty covered with
white crosses to
overwhelm
the book of the dead. She is weeping
bullets
stamped "made in the USA"
like ones left in the bodies of
our soldiers.
Friendly fire?
Arms for Iran. Arms for Iraq.
Violent
cash crop returning to
haunt us.
The nation that prepares for war
finds war.
Prepare for peace.

Some who survive desert hurricanes
bring death back home in diseased
platelets. Battalions of
white corpuscles
can't defeat vaccination cocktails
and depleted uranium
blowing across the earth.
Don't drink the hot chemical
soup formerly known as
diet coke.
Iraq has come back
to the gene bank. Mother's
milk is laced with

Linda Albertano 179

rocket fuel. And a desert
storm veteran named McVeigh
once learned
that all's fair in love
and collateral damage. Remember
when bombs lit Oklahoma
City like the 4th of July over
no-fly zones?

What will it be, America? Scent of cinnamon
and sandalwood? Or stench of
sulphur and seared
flesh? In Washington DC
desert storm sniper
finds busdrivers and suburban
moms in coldblue
gunsight. In Fort Bragg, Carolina,
delta force family values
decree death for wives
of suicidal killing machines. Boys
don't cry. They just
squeeze
triggers of military madness.
Staccato drumroll of
death. Those who prepare for war
will find war. Prepare
for peace!

All over America, veterans live
in trees and in refrigerator
boxes. Holding signs, "have pneumonia...
will work for medicine." 10,000 dead
of desert illness. Populating
prisons and poorhouses.

Princes and queens of Africa.
Royal bloodline of Aztec nations. Noble sons and
daughters of dustbowl
farms. Of mines. Factories. Skin
blackened with coal dust
and axle grease.

Meanwhile,
old men with soft white hands
make life and death
decisions from the safety of
mansions and ranchhouses. Maps of
Newark, Detroit, Chicago, and
Los Angeles are soaked with
vital fluids of
the young. Do not drench the
terrain of Arabia with their
blood.
The nation that prepares
for peace will find peace. Prepare
for peace!

America.
You are a glass house. Your
instruments of battle
are bleeding colors of destruction all
over the globe.
Be the beautiful. Be strong
and brave. Lay down
your weapons. Be the land of
the free. Remember?
How you
lifted your lamp beside
the golden door?

Linda Albertano 181

Unfurl
the great, fluttering promise
you once made
on that tall ship of state.
So that we might
sail
your irresistible amber
waves far,

far
into the future.

KABUL

But Larks have not forgotten to fly
And grass still sprouts from the earth of Kabul
And rivers are replenished by the snows of Pamirs
And the groves of Samangan are filled with sounds of birds
Tahmineh will stand by the road
Unveiled, with gleams of joy in her eyes
And Rostam will dismount Rakhsh
He'll see no ordeal facing him
But love, love only love

Thus the cannons will go silent
and the tanks rust under the green moss
And the soldiers return to their garrisons
And the turbaned to their temples
And the children to their desks
And the country girls will come to the city
Shouting in the alleys:
"Flowers! Flowers! Flowers!"
And the old poet of the city of Toos
Will look toward the east
From the balcony of his garden
And say in the sweet words of Dari:
"Ah, Kabul! Do not suffer any longer
Or shed your blood in vain
Roodabeh will untie her hair again
It will fall from her high balcony
And Zal will rise to his love"

Ferdowsi of Toos, the great Persian epic poet, wrote
Shah Nameh a thousand years ago. In it, Roodabeh, the daughter of
the king of Kabul, gives birth to Rostam, the greatest Iranian
mythical warrior.

VINE

There is a green fence
Between death and me
Covered by an old vine.

When passing by
I part the dense leaves
To see the other side
But the sun blinds me.
I pluck a single leaf
And like an old palmist
Stare at its cryptic lines
Asking myself in silence,
"Who has planted this vine?"
And before people point at me
I brush the dust from my clothes
And go on my way.

DEFINITION OF WAITING

I write about days
I write on its leopard back
accidents that don't take place
names of objects like
eyes of women gazing at the blind afternoon
nights that trace the empty ring in our souls
bland days
ash between fingers
as fragile as
the glass of a voice
holes
immense holes in the pages and in what is said
days drawn by the absence in which we sleep
writing

waiting

—translated from the Spanish by Anthony Seidman

WORLD PICTURE

Far away, a dust column in the storm takes solid form
People leaning against the wind to stay erect
Are like one speechless stature after another
The storm enters its fiercest hour
I have seen so much immobility
That faraway place—how far is it from me after all?
I walk toward it, as if going to my martyrdom, but to
    what end?
Let me disappear into the storm
Behind that giant dust column
Behind those people standing in the storm
Further than far!

Hands that touch the storm cannot be drawn back
Another individual commits himself
The eye of the storm, secret of distance
A crowd turned motionless within the storm
Thrashing, exchanging blows, who can still see it?
Who is still unmoved in the distance?
All have been swept in, unable to leave
All are motionless, have disappeared
I want to raise a cry, who can still hear?
Cries I raised sift earthward like a dust column
Where has the storm gotten to now?

Far away, so much immobility remains
Resembling a picture I cannot move aside
Yet all this is beyond my ability to touch
I am weak, prone to the muteness of this world scene
Its impact keeps me from taking even a step
Too far away, too lacking in aim
The storm's passing leaves me bereft of a goal

The crowd has begun walking, making conversation
Coming and going from houses that just now seemed
    like a backdrop
Myself an individual, outside of the crowd
Within an imagined, unstoppable storm

Such is the tragedy I am ordained to live in
Martyrdom is right here, no need to go far
No one can see, no one can hear
A person's sacrifice is worth something
Because of it, the dust-cloud rises in glory
The crowd-tableau takes on meaning
Myself, a starting point and contributing cause
    of storms
Grill me with questions, stare me down, you in
    the crowd!
I have already shouted my answer
Far away, concealed in the distance of my spirit
Open sky, within silence, won't be stopped from
rising!

—translated from the Chinese by Denis Mair

WOLFMAN

i'm a grappling iron
i'm the miracle in which fear crosses itself
the wound sniffing its own blood and devouring itself
i'm a thread that catches on fire vertically
open up the door

—translated from the Spanish by Anthony Seidman

Vol. 28 No. 2

TRUTH ETC.

the
Constitution & Declaration
belong
to
the
people

not
the
government

Fred Dewey 189

evangelical death squads

rigged elections
communistic fictions

take your pick

the
Constitution & Declaration
the democratic-republic
have been

overthrown

the
Confederacy
won

expanded, modernized, more liberal

the **USA** is an occupied country

a Global **CSA**
(Confederate States
of America)

NSS + cartels + society = total state
everywhere

two-party
dictatorship,
not one

Oh America, land of plenty

**we need
poems
and poets**   **art and artists**

**for
this**

**to
learn
to
speak
and
act**

again,

Vol. 28 No. 2

a
general strike

or two
or a hundred
or a thousand

for the
Constitution & Declaration

for the democratic-republic

for freedom.

Fred Dewey 193

Linda Albertano is a musician, artist, and poet who has performed at the LA Theater Center, the John Anson Ford Theater, Knitting Factory, London's October Gallery, and Amsterdam's One World Poetry Festival. Her CD is *Skin* (Quiet Time) and her work is featured on the Venice Poets Walls, curated by Beyond Baroque.

Ammiel Alcalay is a poet, translator, critic, scholar, activist, and editor. Recent activities include *Poetry Is News* (with Anne Waldman), and the *OlsonNow Project* (with Michael Kelleher). A new book, *scrapmetal*, is forthcoming from Heretical Texts at Factory School (from which the text here is excerpted); a book of essays, *A Little History*, a reprint of his *from the warring factions*, and his co-translation of Syrian poet Faraj Bayrakdar are forthcoming from Beyond Baroque. His previous books include *After Jews and Arabs: Remaking Levantine Culture*, and *Keys to the Garden*, an anthology of contemporary Israeli poetry.

Will Alexander's works include *Exobiology as Goddess, Asia & Haiti, Above the Human Nerve Domain, The Stratospheric Canticles, Towards the Primeval Lightning Field*, and a forthcoming a book of essays, *Singing in Magnetic Hoff Beat*, from Factory School. His visual art has been shown in collections in Berlin, Germany, as well as at Beyond Baroque and other locales.

Michele Costa-Baron, a visual artist, and **Therese Bachand**, a poet, have been collaborating on a series of poem/drawings, one of which is printed here. Bachand's forthcoming book, on Green Integer, is titled *luce a cavallo*.

Daniel Berrigan is a longtime peace activist and poet. The poems here are from *Revelation*, a 1980 prose-poem lecture at the UC Berkeley graduate theological school. Berrigan wrote the play *The Trial of the Catonsville Nine*, which ran on Broadway in 1971 and was made into a movie. His books include *A Sunday in Hell: Fables & Poems* by Daniel Berrigan & Hugh MacDonald, *And the Risen Bread: Selected Poems, The Raft Is Not the Shore: Conversations Toward a Buddhist/Christian Awareness* by Thich Nhat Hanh and Daniel Berrigan, *Prison Poems*, and *Uncommon Prayer*.

Martín Camps is author of the collection *Desierto sol* published by Solar. His poetry has appeared in such publications as *Revista de literatura mexicana contemporánea*,

Alforja, and *Entre Líneas.* He was part of the Dialogue Across Borders weekend at Beyond Baroque in 2004.

Sami Shalom Chetrit is a poet, writer, filmmaker and activist who writes and teaches on culture, society, education, and the Israeli-Palestinian conflict. His books include *Shirim Be'Ashdodit* (Poems in Ashdodian), poetry from 1982 to 2002 (Andalus) and *The Mizrahi Struggle in Israel: 1948-2003* (in Hebrew) published in (Am-Oved/Ofakim Series). He is editor-in-chief of *Kedma–Middle Eastern Gate to Israel.* He has lectured at the Center for the Study of Religion at UCLA. With Eli Hamo he produced the documentary *The Black Panthers (in Israel) Speak.*

Claro is a writer and translator living in Paris. His translations of American authors include Thomas Pynchon, William Vollman, Kathy Acker, Dennis Cooper, and others. He has published several volumes of experimental fiction, including *Chair Electrique,* from which the piece here is excerpted, translated by Brian Evenson and published by Soft Skull as *Electric Flesh.*

Jeanette Clough's books include *Island* (Red Hen) and *Cantatas* (Tebot Bach) and two limited editions, *Celestial Burn* (Sacred Beverage) and *Dividing Paradise* (The Inevitable). She has published in *Colorado Review, Denver Quarterly, Nimrod, Ohio Review, Atlanta Review, Poetrybay.com,* and *Pool.*

Wanda Coleman's books include *The Riot Inside Me: Trials & Tremors* (Godine/ Black Sparrow), *Wanda Coleman–Greatest Hits 1966-2003* (Pudding House), *Ostinato Vamps* (Pitt) and from Black Sparrow, *Mercurochrome: New Poems, Bathwater Wine, Native in a Strange Land: Trials & Tremors, Hand Dance, African Sleeping Sickness, Heavy Daughter Blues: Poems & Stories 1968-1986, Imagoes, and Mambo Hips & Make Believe: A Novel.* Her CD is "High Priestess of Word." Her work is featured on the Venice Poets Walls, curated by Beyond Baroque.

Dorit Cypis is an artist (and mediator) working in photography, performance, installation, sculpture, and social action. Her work has been shown in international and national exhibitions including the Whitney, the Isabella Stewart Gardner Museum in Boston, and the permanent collection of the Walker Art Center.

Jeremiah Day, former artist-in-residence at Beyond Baroque, lives in Amsterdam and has shown at Ellen De Bruijne, the Cubitt, BAK, Utrecht, Expodium, Beyond Baroque, the 2005 Cork Caucus, in Cork, Ireland and "We All Laughed At Christopher Columbus," Stedelijk Museum Bureau Amsterdam and forthcoming at Platform Garanti, Istanbul. His publications include *Portable Memorial* and the 2004 *Beyond Baroque Magazine*.

Fred Dewey is a writer and public space activist. He has published his essays in numerous anthologies, magazines, and newspapers, here and abroad. He co-founded the Neighborhood Councils Movement in Los Angeles and is a curator of public art. He directs Beyond Baroque and founded and edits Beyond Baroque Books.

Diane di Prima co-founded the New York Poets Theatre and Poets Press in New York City, where she co-edited *The Floating Bear* (1961-1969) with Amiri Baraka. Moving to San Francisco, she he took part in the Diggers, wrote *Revolutionary Letters*, her epic poem *Loba, Pieces of a Song* (City Lights), and *Recollections of My Life as a Woman* (Viking). Her work has been translated into at least twenty languages. An expanded edition of *Revolutionary Letters* has been done by Last Gasp.

Christoph Draeger has shown his installations, videos, visual art, and interventions widely across Europe and in the US. His solo and group shows include Paco das Artes, Kunsthalle Sao Paulo, Brazil, Catherine Clark Gallery, San Francisco, Roebling Hall, New York, Centre de l'Image, Contemporain, Geneva, PS 1/MOMA, Heidelberger Kunstverein, Heidelberg, MassMoca, and many others, including, most recently, Susanne Vielmetter Projects, Los Angeles.

Estrella del Valle b. 1971 is the author of *La cortesana de Dannan* (Instituto Veracruzano de la Cultura), and her work has appeared in numerous journals. She was part of the Dialogue Across Borders weekend at Beyond Baroque in 2004.

Simone Forti is an internationally recognized dancer and choreographer. Her books include *Handbook in Motion* (Nova Scotia), *Oh, Tongue* (Beyond Baroque), and *Unbuttoned Sleeves* (Beyond Baroque). She has performed extensively in France, around Europe and in Japan. Her recent performances in Los Angeles have been at RedCat and Highways. Forti is recipient of a 2005 Guggenheim Fellowship.

Sesshu Foster's most recent book is *Atomic Aztex*, from City Lights. He is author of *City Terrace Field Manual* and a forthcoming book of poems, *American Loneliness*, from Beyond Baroque.

Amélie Frank founded The Sacred Beverage Press with poet Matthew Niblock. She is author of *A Resilient Heart and OtherVisceral Comforts*, *Flame and Loss of Breath* (Inevitable), *Drink Me* (with Matthew Niblock,, VCP), and *Doing Time on Planet Billy Bob* (1996, Laguna Poets).

Charlene Geisler is a poet and artist, age nine, living in Los Angeles.

Jean-Luc Godard is one of the world's foremost filmmakers, artists, and innovators. His recent films include *Notre Music* and *In Praise of Love*, *Forever Mozart*, *Germany Year Zero*, *JLG/JLG*, and others. He is the subject of a major show at the Pompidou Center in Paris and his books include *Histoire du Cinema*. The excerpt here is from a forthcoming Beyond Baroque single volume translation of texts titled after his most recent films, published by POL in Paris, and translated by Bill Kron.

Jason Greenwald is a writer living in Los Angeles.

Gordon Henderson is a graphic artist living in Los Angeles

Jack Hirschman has recently published a complete, bilingual volume of *The Arcanes* with Multimedia Edizione, in Italy. He is San Francisco Poet-Laureate and has published numerous translations and works of poetry, including *Front Lines*, with City Lights, *A Correspondence of Americans* (Indiana), *Black Alephs* (Trigram), *Lyripol* (City Lights), *The Bottom Line* (Curbstone), and *Endless Threshold* (Curbstone). He edited an anthology on art and activism, *Art On The Line* (Curbstone). He assists in editing *Left Curve* and is a correspondent for *The People's Tribune*.

Anna Krenz established the Zero Project Gallery in Berlin in 2003 to provide a meeting place for artists and others, between West and East, across the Atlantic, and around the world. She writes for Polish architectural magazines and her work focuses on media, journalism, and design. Her show in Berlin in 2005 was *Polish Wife* and she has featured collaborations between LA artist Jim Macinich and Berlin artist Roland Sheferski.

Meng Lang was founding editor of *Haishang*, an underground journal in Shanghai during the '80s. In 1992 he won the "Readers's Prize" from Modern Chinese Poetry, a journal backed by an alliance of underground groups. His poetry collections are: *One Living in This Century* (Lijiang, Guangzhou), *Even the Sunrise is Stale* (Tangshan, Taipei), and *A Child in the Sky* (Ziluolan, Hong Kong). His articles on literature have been published *Mingbao Monthly, Literary Century*, and *World Journal Weekly*. For years he organized exhibitions at the Chinese Cultural Center in Boston. He divides his time between Hong Kong and Boston.

Yan Li joined with Bei Dao in underground writing activities during China's Cultural Revolution, contributed to the original *Today* magazine, and was a member of the Star-Star Group during the Democracy Wall period (1979-1981). His apartment in New York with composer Tan Dun served as a salon for emigre Chinese artists in the late '80s. He edited and published *First LineYihang*, a journal-in-exile and his collections include *This Poem Is Probably Not Bad* (Shulin, Taiwan) and *Spinning Mirror* (Qinghai People's Press), and *Sharing a Pillow with New York* (Shanghai Literature). His work has been published in *The Portable Lower East Side, Manoa* and *Trafika*. His painting was in the Paris Biennial and is in the Shanghai Museum of Modern Art.

David Lloyd, Dublin born, lives in Los Angeles, teaching at the University of Southern California. Writer and critic, he has published four books of poetry: *Taropatch* (Jimmy's House of Knowledge), *Coupures* (hardPressed Poetry), *Change of State* (Cusp), and *Sill* (Cusp).

Philomene Long is poet laureate of Venice, CA. She is author of *Queen of Bohemia* (Lummox), *Cold Eye Burning at 3:00AM* (Lummox), *American Zen Bones* (Beyond Baroque), and, with her husband John Thomas, *Bukowski in the Bathtub, Great Zen Masters & Other Holy Fools, Ghosts of Venice West* (all Raven), and *Book of Sleep* (Momentum). Her films include *The Beats: An Existential Comedy*, and *The California Missions*. Her work appears in the *Outlaw Bible of American Poetry* and is featured on the Venice Poets Walls, curated by Beyond Baroque.

Édgar Rincón Luna is author of *Aqui comienza la noche interminable published by Tierra Adentro, Par / ten* (Solar), and his work appeared in the anthology *El silencio de lo que cae* (University of Mexico). He was part of the Dialogue Across Borders weekend at Beyond Baroque in 2004.

David Meltzer's recent books include *SF Beat: Talking with the Poets* (City Lights), *David's Copy, Selected Poems* (Penguin) and *David Meltzer: Poetry With Jazz*. With Steve Dickison, he co-edits *Shuffle Boil*, a highly irregular journal about music written by poets, writers, musicians. He teaches at New College of California.

Keith Morris is lead singer for Midget Handjob and was singer with the Circle Jerks and other LA bands. He was lead singer in the original Black Flag.

Majid Naficy has published two collections of poetry, *Muddy Shoes* (Beyond Baroque) and *Father and Son* (Red Hen) as well as a doctoral dissertation *Modernism and Ideology in Persian Literature* (University Press of America). He is co-editor of the literary organ of Iranian Writers' Association in Exile and the author of more than twenty books in Persian. He fled Iran in 1983. His work is featured on the Venice Poets Walls, curated by Beyond Baroque.

Rich Nielsen is an artist who lives and works in LA.

Gaspar Orozco is author of *Abrir fuego*, published by Tierra Adentro (from which the work here is excerpted). His work has appeared in *Alforja* and *Letras Libres*. He was part of the Dialogue Across Borders weekend at Beyond Baroque in 2004.

Sotirios Pastakas has published four volumes of poetry in Greece: *To Athoryvo gegonos* (The noiseless Event), *I Mathisi tis Anapnois* (Learning of Breath), 1990, 1999 and 2001, and more recently *O Koinonos ton Apostaseon* (The commutator of the distances), and *Nisos Chios* (The Island of Chios).

Eric Priestley is author of the novel *Raw Dog* and the poetry collection *Abracadabra*. He is a journalist and was a member of the Watts Writers Workshop. His work was featured in *Beyond Baroque Magazine* (2004).

Lucas Reiner is a painter living in Los Angeles. He has shown his work in Europe, New York, and Los Angeles. His monograph with Beyond Baroque is *Trees & Words*.

Naomi Replansky published her first book, *Ring Song*, in 1952 and, after many years, returned to print with *The Dangerous World*. Her work has been celebrated by George Oppen, Harvey Shapiro, and Grace Paley. She has worked as a lathe operator, office worker, computer programmer, and teacher.

Yi Sha, winner of *Poetry Reference Magazine's* Ten-Year Prize, is one of the most controversial poets in China. His work was originally influenced by Bei Dao and other Misty generation poets. His first collection was *Starve the Poets*. He edited *A Modern Book of Odes*, a popular anthology of free verse in Chinese, and he is Chinese translator of Charles Bukowski. As moderator for the "Tang Website Forum," he spearheaded polemics between the "populist writing" and the "intellectual writing" camps in current Chinese poetry.

Sue Spaid, in fall 2005, drove across 36 states, presenting lectures on art and philosophy at various venues including Beyond Baroque. From 1990-1995, she owned Sue Spaid Fine Art. She was Curator at Cincinnati's Contemporary Arts Center from 1999-2002, where she curated *Ecovention: Current Art to Transform Ecologies* (and edited a book of the same title, published 2002, by the Contemporary Art Center, www.greenmuseum.org, ecoartspace) along with other groundbreaking shows. She has published columns in *Art & Text* and *ArtUS*.

Annette Sugden is an artist and writer living in Los Angeles.

Judith Taylor is author of *Curios* (Sarabande) and *Dreams of the Animal Kingdom* (Zoo) and editor of *Pool* magazine.

John Thomas moved to Venice, CA and the Beat Scene in 1959, after living in the East and visiting many times with Ezra Pound at Saint Elizabeth's. His books include *Feeding the Animal* (Lummox), *Nevertheless* (Illuminati), *John Thomas* and *Epopoeia and the Decay of Satire* (both Red Hill). His work is featured in the *Outlaw Bible of American Poetry*. With his wife Philomene Long, he co-wrote

Bukowski in the Bathtub, Great Zen Masters & Other Holy Fools, Ghosts of Venice West (all Raven), and *Book of Sleep* (Momentum). His work is featured on the Venice Poetry Walls, curated by Beyond Baroque.

Marguerite Waller co-edited *Frontline Feminisms: Women, War, and Resistance* (Routledge), *Dialogue and Difference: Feminisms Challenge Globalization* (Palgrave), and *The Wages of Empire: Neoliberal Policies, Armed Repression, and Women's Poverty* (Paradigm, forthcoming). She was a member of the women's art-making collective, *Las Comadres*, in the early nineties in the San Diego/Tijuana border region. "The Language of Globalization" is from a longer piece in *Social Identities* (Sept. 06).

Poet and writer **Tyler Williams** is completing his degree at UC Berkeley. He worked in the Beyond Baroque archive before moving to San Francisco.

Genevieve Yue is an artist, designer, and writer living in Los Angeles.

A LITTLE ABOUT BEYOND BAROQUE

Beyond Baroque is one of the United States' leading independent Literary/Arts Centers and public spaces dedicated to literary and cultural production, contact, interaction, and community building. Founded in 1968, it is based in the Old Town Hall in Venice, California, near the Pacific Ocean. It offers a program of readings, free workshops, publishing, bookstore, archiving, and education. Its Wednesday Free Poetry Workshop is possibly the longest continuously running such free workshop in the country. The Center began on Abbot Kinney Blvd, nearby, and moved into its permanent home on Venice Blvd. in 1980.

The Center's mission is experimentation in and preservation of literature in dialogue with all the arts and humanities. Public space and culture-building has been a central part of all its activities.

*

Literary & Arts Programming
The Center's Reading Series is one of the country's oldest, most respected literary series, supporting local and internationally prominent writers and new and emerging writers. The Center offers an Open Reading series, as well as New Music, Film, Dance, and Performance, panels and lectures.

Free Workshops and Education
The center offers year-round free weekly workshops in poetry, fiction, non-fiction, and screenwriting open to people of all ages and economic, racial, and cultural backgrounds and origins.

Bookstore & Archive
Beyond Baroque's Bookstore and Archive emphasize new and overlooked poetry and fiction, small press books, self-published chapbooks, and 'zines. The Archive collects and preserves works. The chapbook collection features self-published, limited-run and one-of-a-kind works. A catalog of the chapbook archive is now online.

Beyond Baroque Books

The Center launched its own imprint, Beyond Baroque Books, in 1998, dedicated to emerging, overlooked, out of print and experimental writing, as well as the history and legacy of experimental and alternative writing, poetry, and the arts in Los Angeles.

Residencies, Collaborations, and Public Art

Beyond Baroque features residencies and collaborations with writers and writers' groups from around the region and country. Center-curated public art projects include permanent poetry installations such as the lobby of the Junipero State Office Building in Downtown LA and the Venice Poetry Walls, featuring poets from Venice past and present.

Project Room

Beyond Baroque's Project Room features shows by emerging curators, artists, and art with an emphasis on experimental text and its relation to the visual arts.

Membership and Support

Beyond Baroque relies on the generous support of those who believe in its mission. New members and volunteers are encouraged to contact us.

Call (310) 822-3006 for more information.

JOIN US AND BECOME A MEMBER OR VOLUNTEER!

A Place Dedicated to the Possibilities of Language
Fred Dewey, Director

BEYOND BAROQUE BOOKS

Fred Dewey, ed. *TRUTH Etc. Beyond Baroque Vol 28 #2* $5
Simone Forti, Terrence Luke Johnson, Sarah Swenson, Douglas
   Wadle *Unbuttoned Sleeves* $8
Benjamin Hollander *Vigilance* $12
Fred Dewey, ed. *Beyond Baroque Vol. 26 #2* $5
Lucas Reiner *Trees & Words* $5
K. Curtis Lyle *Electric Church* $12
Simone Forti *Oh, Tongue* $12
Ammiel Alcalay *from the warring factions* $12
Nancy Agabian *Princess Freak* $10
Philomene Long *American Zen Bones: Maezumi Roshi Stories* $10
Majid Naficy *Muddy Shoes* $8
Michael Datcher, ed. *Black Love* $8
Jessica Pompei, Holiday Mason, Sarah Maclay, eds. *Echo 681
   Beyond Baroque Wednesday Poetry Workshop* $8
Eve Wood *Paper Frankenstein* $5
Joel Brouwer *This Just In* $5
Sandor Tádjèck / Kurt Brown *A Voice In The Garden* $5

PREVIOUS PUBLICATIONS

Terry Wolverton & Benjamin Weissman, eds. *Harbinger: Fiction
   and Poetry by Los Angeles Writers* (with the L.A. Festival) $8
Benjamin Weissman, Paul Vangelisti, Amy Gerstler, Don Suggs,
   Lane Relyea, eds. *FOREHEAD, Vol's 1 & 2,* $7 each
Chinese Folk Poetry, translated by Cecilia Liang $4

*For orders & distribution, please contact Small Press Distribution
(SPD) at (800) 869-7553 or at www.SPDbooks.org.*